ACTING ON PURPOSE

By

IAN CHAMPION

First published by www.lulu.com 2007

Printed in the United States by
www.lulu.com

10 9 8 7 6 5 4 3 2 1

ISBN 978-1-84799-907-8

This is my first book. It won't be my last (unless irate villagers with burning torches march on Castle Champion)

Grateful thanks are due to these inspiring people:

My parents, for the gift of their unconditional love and support over the years (especially when they couldn't relate to what I was doing)

Heather, Chris, Josh and Tim for their love, encouragement and humour

Andrew - and other friends past and present

Shaun, for going first and then helping me up the mountain…

Tony and Patrick, for representing me so well

Dr Wayne Dyer and Napoleon Hill

The Stones and the Who

~Bless you all ~

CONTENTS

PROLOGUE

I s there anyone more attractive to an actor than a fellow performer who radiates confidence? There is nothing more compelling than an artist, or indeed anyone, who is fully in command of themselves, who walks and talks from an inner knowing of their place and purpose. Audiences adore them and believe them; colleagues are drawn to them and trust them – and so do employers.

Acting On Purpose, as its name suggests, is about enabling the actor to work and live from a clear inner direction. I want to help you focus your desire and commitment, and then carry out that purpose in dynamite auditions and attitudes. In a sense, I'll show you how to get the job *before* you get the job! You may have felt real confidence before now; or it may have seemed like a frail and unreliable companion who came along and left when it felt like it. Ever had that feeling?

I'm not writing this book to teach fake bravado or manufacture passion and commitment where it doesn't exist in you. Those tricks are easily spotted and the effects don't last. They insult your audience and cheapen you. This is about releasing more effectively the talent you already have. I'm assuming you have talent. You may not be gifted, but if you're blessed with the unstoppable will to act, learn and grow to be the best artist you can be, that is incredibly potent *potentially*...

I've aimed the writing at actors of all levels and experience, covering the personal (professional training and ongoing practices of mind and body) through to the public (your CV, effective relationships with an agent, superior audition technique) and a healthy approach to the business in general. No matter what the subject though, every chapter is underpinned by the same principle: reflecting nothing less than the very best in you.

This book is written in a very direct way. Woolly-mindedness and timidity are the most common weaknesses in actors who aren't getting anywhere. The frustrated ones usually aren't lazy -they are often full of passion and energy. The trouble is they either don't know what they really want, or are afraid to go after it with full belief. Deep down, they don't believe it is their right or purpose to be on that stage or in front of that camera. It's that missing total conviction that the successful ones have, that enables success and long-term survival. Without it, you have no magnetism to convince others and the plans you do make dissolve like New Year resolutions. Shatter these barriers and the dam will burst, sending this pent-up hydro power flowing powerfully through whichever channels you set yourself.

Anyone who tells you that a successful career in the arts by its nature is simply a product of randomness, fate or just luck is not telling the whole truth. The ones who failed will use this propaganda for comfort in the pub. The successful ones often keep quiet about how much they intended and willed their success to happen in advance. Attractive modesty prevails, but the reality is far more compelling.

Acting On Purpose is a way of approaching the business that is not about vague hopes and 'leaving it to chance'. It involves passion, brains and focus. When asked what took him to the top, film producer Dino De Laurentiis pointed to his head, his heart and his nether regions. Like a caring friend or relative, life can only be expected to give us what we ask of it. If we ask timidly for very little, anticipating mostly misery and rejection along the way, we will surely get it. When we ask for more, doing it boldly, clearly and asking more of ourselves in assisting it, then life obeys that too.

My intentions are to challenge and inspire you to the heights of your potential. I'm not stridently demanding these techniques are the only way to do it, but they work for me. Since I began to apply what I'm learning with faith, the rewards have been increasingly gratifying.

Try out my suggestions. You might even find some of the approaches useful in other areas of your life as well. There is nothing to lose except fear.

CHAPTER 1
YOU

Why do you want to be an actor?

This is a question you'll be asked many times in your career. You may well ask it of yourself during a long dark night of the soul when things aren't going according to plan. Your desire right now might seem so obvious you've never questioned it. I suggest you do examine it from time to time, if only to reaffirm that your actions are taking you in the direction you really want to go. Your answer may change as your understanding of yourself and your life evolves over time. However, the emotional fire, the basic need to express oneself in this way should always be stoked and protected. This is the core that you can always return to; if it burns brightly enough to keep you on the path.

Can you rely on your passion for acting even when you can't rely on it financially? Are you sure that you can support it even when it doesn't appear to be supporting you? This is one test of integrity. The life of an actor is made up of peaks and troughs which all have to be ridden. We can get so consumed by the lure of the visual trappings, glamorous photo opportunities, the received idea of fame and the material prosperity on offer. We sometimes forget that these are all actually side effects to the main purpose, which is the love of the work itself.

Addressing your own guiding principles as an actor has never been more important than at this time in the arts. Instant 'celebrity' on offer via televised talent and reality shows tempts the good and the lousy to bypass any craft and the building of sound resolve. Instead, the chance to be so easily thrust into a sudden end-result of fame without preparation of character encourages a lack of respect for the very qualities that will keep you level-headed.

Many celebrated stars turn into black holes as quickly as they first shine. They achieve recognition so suddenly that they've not had time to develop a long-term work ethic and respect for their talent that those who forge great longevity come from. Whether you're young or old, new or a veteran of acting, take the opportunity to reflect on where you are now. Hone your capabilities and appreciate the integrity of who has gone before you and what it took from you to get you here. You'll have a much surer platform for weathering the storms and staying firm in the long run.

Someone once said that everyone should aim to become a millionaire. Not for the money, (this is simply a nice end-product), but for what it will take of your character to achieve it. I think you'll agree a person who makes a million is far more interesting than one who is given it for very little in return.

The pursuit of definite goals where the expression and development of you is the main drive will forge character in you that is more enduring than the temporary trinkets. You will also feel far more fulfilled even when the results aren't quite what you expect. This way, when you are granted the fulfilment of your dreams, I daresay you will be grateful and then respectfully set the bar again to a greater challenge, rather than collapsing into the ruin of the ill-prepared and shallow.

Many performers (not just actors) get into show-business for the wrong reasons. The business of show is making it your business to put yourself 'on show'. Let's face it, at its very core it's a public need for more attention than you would normally get or deserve. Put like that it might sound awfully selfish but all art is expression and it's no less valid for being something you feel compelled to do. When acting is done well, it matters because it illuminates the human condition, inspires us and can give us a bloody good laugh at ourselves as well. That takes a particular kind of sensibility: it's not just the putting on of hats and 'acting daft' or being admired for a glamorous appearance.

Hyde and seek

To act is a willingness to be vulnerable, risking and encouraging self-exposure. The more you dare reveal of yourself truthfully, the more you succeed in reflecting the audience. Curiously our profession attracts many practitioners who in real life would seem the most unlikely people to carry this out. Rather than the loud extrovert clown that people assume an actor must be, there are plenty who are quite shy reclusive individuals when not performing. Some actors in normal life, like many who are introverted, are quite inhibited but have a huge compulsion to express themselves at the same time. Luckily in show business we have the outlet of performance to satisfy this need. As ironic as it sounds, as long as the conditions are controlled we can become immensely free and confident. The most acclaimed theatre actor of the last century, Sir Laurence Olivier, was said to be very much like this: a private and somewhat uncertain person 'in his own skin' off-stage yet in-role could unleash an incredibly dynamic force of sheer exhibitionism.

Perhaps this Jeckyll and Hyde duality describes you and you're finding it difficult to come to terms with it. I recognise this in myself. Lord knows I wouldn't do some of the strange things I've enacted on camera or stage in real life – and having that freedom is part of the point of being an actor for me. If you share this conflict, your secret is safe with me. Accept it and make peace with it and it will also be safe within you. Recognise that just like the good Doctor in the story, your burning desire to express even the ugliest part of yourself is connected to who you really are and is nothing to be ashamed of. (That's not to say I'm advocating a full-scale crime wave of unfettered psyches, mind you). Unlike Dr Jeckyll, you can release your full creativity in acting at no cost to anyone – and have fun doing it.

Attention and approval

One of the most seductive sirens steering actors to the treacherous rocks is their relationship with the need for attention. A spell in a rehabilitation clinic seems to be such a commonplace stopping-off point in showbiz that it's almost expected as a career move. At the root of a lot of it is an inability to cope with either an excess of attention, or the sudden lack of it after long exposure to unrealistic adoration. Attention and approval is potentially a self-image altering drug that intoxicates when it's there and can cause devastating pain when it's taken away again.

A youth who was neglected may very well seek attention in abnormal quantities later in life from a great number of people as a performer. Theirs is a deep-seated craving to fill a painful void in their lives through performing. The good news is that for some this can be corrected through good relationships and therapy, and even for some through a healthy approach to a showbiz career.

Sadly for some this thirst can't just be slaked by the occasional blast of *Mustang Sally* on the karaoke down the local. The greed for approval can be such that it causes intense trauma whether it is met or not. In other words, if they are fed a gargantuan meal of public praise they weren't prepared for, the overload can be so overwhelming that they need to be taken away for private treatment. Equally, there is the potentially self-destructive consequence of a performer who comes to rely on public adulation for a falsely inflated sense of themselves, and then implodes when the public transfers its fickle attention to another.

Either way, if you have enough self-knowledge to know your greatest need in life is a compulsion to fill a huge gap of missing attention, a career as an actor may be a mistake. Rarely would achieving fame ever be enough to fulfil you. Public recognition is as unreliable and unfathomable as the weather reports. People's tastes change; your self-acceptance need not.

Stop reading this for a moment and spread one of your palms open across your chest. Breathe deeply in and out against your hand. Feel your heartbeat. That's the only constant approval that can ever be truly relied upon: the compass of your inner self. If you go within and understand another way of gaining the inner comfort you need, I advise you to take it. You may save yourself and those around you many years on a destructive path.

If however, your passion to communicate as a performer is genuine, for the love of doing it for itself, then welcome to a profession unlike most others.

Inner confidence

To survive as an actor, you need a very strong sense of self from within. During your career, you will hear many changing opinions about yourself. If you don't have this strong inner compass, you're in for a life of feeling like a leaf blowing in the wind. Flexibility to changing circumstances and plans is healthy. Allowing the course of your life to be dictated by other people, however, means you have no firm personal base from which to judge anything. This is what you must develop and trust if you are to cope with fluctuating demands and emotion.

If your confidence is externally-directed, depending almost entirely on the opinions of others, you'll constantly veer between the high of acceptance for a part and the low point of feeling rejected or exploited by employers. I find roller-coasters exhilarating, but I don't recommend them as a way of life unless you can find one that just keeps going upward! Externally-directed folk are also prey to jealousy of their partners or friends when the other person has a job coming up and they don't. They are only happy if validated by other people and their success in comparison and this can lead to the self-delusions above. Not the healthiest point of view is it?

Instead, how about cultivating a sense of your own value and contribution that is unique to you and you alone; one that is continually supported by your own inner confidence and approval, not dependent on what others believe or achieve? This is what it means to be internally-directed. If you don't get picked for a part, it doesn't matter. You may not know why you were turned down. If you do and it's something you can work on, do it. Alternately, the reasons may be so disconnected from you that it needn't be taken seriously. You may have looked like the director's ex-wife. Maybe they wanted a blonde-haired guy instead of a brunette. Since we are all too ready to believe reasons that feed self doubt, we might just as well believe valid ones that leave our happiness intact. Shrug, smile, go home and forget about it till the next one.

An actor is always learning to be better. The only failure you can have is an experience you didn't learn from.

Operating from knowing

If you want to get a good score in a darts match, how successful are you going to be wearing a blindfold, facing the wrong way or throwing the darts with the lights turned off? The same applies to your success as an actor. When you're focused on where you're aiming your desires, you'll hit the target a damn sight more easily. It takes discipline of mind and steadfastness to work on naming your desire, your plan to carry it out and then taking the steps to make that a reality.

The recent rise in 'instant fame' TV talent shows is a great accelerator for those with talent and the strong work ethic. However, it also attracts time-wasters who usually reveal themselves before they even sing! You've seen the self-deluded ones who stand before the panel of judges and emote unashamedly about how this is "The only thing I've ever wanted to do. It's the only thing I'm good at", with the kind of desperate gush that only a skilled plumber should face. There is no credibility behind their words. It is emotion shouting loudly to impress where the ability does not.

Have you noticed how when the real talent comes in, you can sense the difference sometimes without them even opening their mouths? They come in knowing what they want. There's a sense of it already being worked out and thought-through to some extent. Yes, it's raw and untutored in its energy and presentation, yet a performer worth your time knows what is worth their time – and it's not cringe-worthy self-promotion. They let their talent speak for them. They use fewer words to sell themselves because they've already decided what they want and only need to communicate that.

Ironically, they are also the ones who know how to handle rejection. They may disagree and 'reject the rejection' inside, but outside will accept it economically and with grace. Like a mature sporting professional, they will leave the field with dignity, knowing that pleading with a referee is demeaning and never reverses a decision against them anyway. For me, it's a joy to witness that kind of talent and sense of self-worth, and help to nurture it where I can. The rest is a waste of everyone's time.

In his memoirs *Rewrites*, Neil Simon remembers his ex-wife, actress Marsha Mason, accompanying him to a theatre to watch him hold auditions for his latest Broadway play. She decided to sit apart from Simon and his producer as they deliberated and record her own views on each auditionee.

She would then compare notes with the other two afterwards. She had never spectated at an audition process before, having always been one of the hopefuls on stage. What she observed from a judge's point of view was a common thread in how actors behave – and it was a revelation to her. It was no surprise that her decisions tallied almost exactly with the two men. She said afterwards it was as though the chosen actors actually picked themselves. He agreed, feeling that somehow the right actor comes onto the stage and invites the decision-maker to "Relax. Stop looking. Just trust that the part belongs to me". Hiring professionals know when they are meeting someone who has that inner knowledge.

So how do you acquire it? Can you acquire it? Or is that innate security something you have to be born with? If it was, there'd be no point in my writing this book. There are practitioners in every walk of life who don't need to examine their motives and confidence, yet all of us need to clarify our intentions and plans once in a while, if only to regularly check we are getting what we originally asked for.

Types of work:

Boards and clapper-boards

Some actors have a very definite preference for either theatre or screen. Others do not; they simply want to learn to act full-stop and are open to all avenues. Is it necessary to choose? I don't believe you have to feel you must select one branch and stay with it for good to succeed in this business. Many actors find their niche in one discipline because it simply happened that way or because their first love was guided by vivid childhood memories of the magic of film or stage rather than a career plan. Neither need determine a rigid course that you can't adapt and deviate from. Follow what you love – change and development is part of a focused strategy.

A healthy-minded artist never stops evolving. If you trained purely in theatre for three years and want to develop screen skills, you can simply gain extra training to adapt to the demands of a new medium. There are evening classes, film school courses for camera acting technique, the practical experience of short independent films etc. A camera actor can expand into theatre, being mindful that it's broader, freer arena of expression must be respected and learned.

You may have a single-minded yearning to work in one area of the business and have no interest in diversifying. If so, then go to it and commit with joy and purpose to the training that directly supports this. For those whose love of acting is all-embracing as to the variety of possible work, allow me to suggest excelling in both screen and theatre. Aside from greater confidence and commercial flexibility, the two methods do actually compliment and benefit each other. There are many benefits in gaining and experiencing both skills sets.

For instance, on face value a play and film script look deceptively similar. They are both laid out as sparse character lines on the page rather than the dense descriptive text of a book. On closer inspection the technical demands on the actor are actually different. Scenes written for film and TV are usually much shorter than in theatre, featuring very lean dialogue exchanges and quick transfers between locations. (With the exception of screenwriters like Quentin Tarantino who celebrate language and allow elaborate dialogue). Such a strongly visual medium often requires the action be kept moving through image as much as dialogue.

Consequently screen performers without stage experience are very unused to crafting the emotional shape and stamina within a long continuous speech. Sadly this creates a confidence crisis for them when these opportunities approach such as in a film faithfully adapted from a stage play. They may have to do unnecessarily short broken-up takes that render the flow of the big speech harder to sew together cohesively and ends up as a less effective whole.

For the theatre animal, the spoken word is king. Scene changes are a lot less frequent, so conflict is by necessity explored in lengthier verbal encounters between characters. Stage actors therefore are much more accustomed to expressing the big speech. Give a film monologue to a dual exponent of stage and screen and they relish the chance to get some serious camera-hogging time and strut their stuff. I once had to do a page-and-a-half court case summation in a film and was allowed to perform the speech in complete runs from every angle to gain emotional momentum.

Screen acting training can assist in stage rehearsals where you have to 'retake' a section many times, sometimes for technical reasons, using the intense short bursts of concentration typical of screen work. When running through a sequence repeatedly within a play, I think of each attempt as a separate 'take'. This keeps it fun and creative and prevents the monotony of repetition from creeping in.

Exposure to performing an entire play nightly enables the actor to see the overview of a character's journey and the meaning of a whole piece rather than just as bite-sized sequences. This can be very helpful with TV and film scripts that are usually shot out of chronological order. You need to know beforehand how your character develops in the bigger overall picture because you may shoot a vital climactic scene from later very early on in the schedule.

Probably the greatest separation between the two disciplines is in the scale of an actor's performance. This varies immensely between expression for the intimacy of the camera and the broad arena of a stage. Being able to vary between extreme precision and dynamic physical presence gives extra juice to that showing-off drive inside many performers. The one-ring circus becomes more; not just "Look at me" but "Watch me do this too!"

An actor that has only trained in cinema or TV may find it slightly daunting to fill a large stage space, yet its relative freedom of expression is often an exhilarating change. For the camera, precise physical placings (called 'marks') have to be adhered to otherwise you disappear out of the frame. Also the emotive energy is internalized much more to suit the delicacy of being magnified by the lens. On the other hand, theatre allows a freer reign of the full instrument of the actor – the fulsome breathing technique needed to carry the voice further and the expressive use of the whole body in the character.

This is not to say that either is a superior art form. As a director in both fields, Jonathan Miller once observed in an interview that he felt modern theatre acting is becoming influenced by the subtlety of film. Before the invention of cinema, there was only the declamatory overblown theatrical style such as that of Sir Henry Irving. Miller is suggesting that nowadays stage performances are more naturalistic, powerfully drawing the audience in as much as projecting outward. Transferred to film, as long as the theatre actor is skilled at reducing expression (but not intensity) there is enormous riveting power in seeing all that seething emotion reigned in under the lens.

There's always been an unfair perception that stage acting is somehow more 'legitimate' than film. The obvious far greater financial rewards in motion pictures are judged as subtracting credibility from its content, as though existing on lower wages, (starving for one's art?) in low-end theatre always produces art of greater integrity. The principal reason given for this prejudice though is that theatre is a pure actor's medium; all one's technical skills and shortcomings are nakedly on display to others without any artificial enhancement. Admittedly screen performances can be doctored in post-production to cover glaring flaws such as poor pacing, a weak voice or the lack of sufficient talent to create simple reactions without repeated attempts. However, total mastery of body, mind and focused energy 'in the now' is not just the province of live performance. Try hitting the emotional peak of an argument out of nowhere on camera, and then repeating it afresh twenty times due to errors that aren't your fault. You never know which take will finally be used so you have to get it right *every time*.

Ultimately I hope that my enthusiasm for transferring between both screen and stage comes across, and as impartially as possible. Let's not forget that versatility in the modern actor's box of tricks increases your employment potential. You are as likely to be offered a few lines in a lucrative TV cameo as you are to take on a theatre tour. If you decide to stick to one type of work and not aim to master others, then at least your hand isn't forced by worry over lack of experience. After all, instilling confidence is part of the purpose of this book.

Whilst I focus on targeting mainstream work that is financially lucrative or at least sustaining, there is much to be gained from jobs where the pay is low but the satisfaction and potential for growth can be high (as long as you observe points of caution along the way). Here, I'll discuss the particular environments of Theatre-In-Education, Forum Theatre, Profit-Share Theatre and the world of Independent Film. Many actors opt for making their creative home in specific niches of the business like these.

Theatre-In-Education

Theatre-In-Education (T.I.E.) is theatre that explores issues concerning young people, performed in an educational setting. Rather than pure performance, they involve techniques for interacting with their audience such as role-play, simulations, workshops, and Forum Theatre (see below). Since the work is based on issues relevant to young people's experiences (such as racism, bullying, sexual education etc), its function is to actively involve and challenge young people's views and behaviour. The audience are encouraged to be honest and open, exploring and playing others' points of view. As you can imagine, this has great potential for positive influence in society and is a strong reason for many actors coming into the business. Many drama training colleges in recent years offer courses that focus on theatre in the community in this way.

Forum Theatre

Forum is also a form of educational theatre, developed in the 1960s by Brazilian theatre director Augusto Boal. He believed theatre could be a platform for teaching people strategies to change their world. Forum is designed to make people more aware of problems they may have not considered previously in society or their workplace. Its audiences may be a cross section of society, or employees or end-users of particular organisations and social services. Its scenarios are aimed at stimulating audience participation through discussion, interactive role-playing and shared experiences.

In a typical forum workshop, often there is a central character that undergoes a 'revolving door' experience of going from one scenario to the next, encountering conflicts along the way. What makes Forum unique in theatre is that audience members are invited to stop the action at any point and come forward to demonstrate a solution by intervening on a character's behalf. They may offer to replace the main character, making their feelings known more clearly and emandeeringly, or to replace an antagonistic problem character to demonstrate how this person may behave more effectively and sensitively to the main person's needs. After the forum scene has been worked through, discussion can take place about the scene's issues. This can be very rewarding not just to the audience but also the actor. I've learned a lot about the needs of many groups in society and how various education and employment bodies function through Forum. Also, the creativity and alertness of adapting to a changing 'unscripted' scenario can be excellent practise and great fun. Actors who thrive on the improvisatory level would enjoy this form of theatre.

For the actor considering these kinds of work, it's important to be realistic about the benefits. The audience (and the actor)'s education is enriched and the satisfaction from letters, drawings and verbal feedback made by participants after a workshop is tremendously heartening. However, this should be where your expectation ends. All too often, actors undertake certain jobs deceiving themselves about where they might lead.

Forum and T.I.E Theatre do NOT lead to mainstream theatre work.

If this is what you are hoping for, and it's the reason you are doing it, stop that application! You will become disillusioned and will do the employing company a disservice. Forum and T.I.E. theatre work can be arduous.

Imagine getting up very early, travelling potentially long distances, loading and unloading a van of equipment for a show – and in harsh wintry conditions. What keeps such actors motivated is the value of the work itself, not a misguided sense of where it may help *their* career.

The pay is also usually Equity minimum, which rules out many people who have a mortgage to pay on their own. On that point, please note that some companies do not offer Equity union contracts. If so, ask around for ex-company members' feedback on their practises and reputation before signing a contract. Without union protection, you may find yourself heavily exploited, and will only have yourself to blame if you willingly enter an unpleasant engagement.

If your circumstances can afford this level of commitment, and you have the desire to do the work for its own sake, then you're a perfect candidate and can look forward to a potentially rewarding experience.

Profit-Share Theatre

Profit-Share Theatre means agreeing to do a show where the actor's rehearsal and performances are only paid if the production is deemed by it's producers to have gone 'into profit'. There is a type of halfway-house where a company finds enough funding to pay for a series of performances or a tour, but not for the rehearsals, so they ask actors to rehearse for free but be paid for performance - knowing sometimes the rehearsal period can be longer than the performance.

Either way, this is an engagement that should only be entered into by an actor with a realistic understanding of what should and should not be expected as there is more at stake than with the above theatre projects.

The Pro's:

*It can be a good opportunity to be seen by potential agents and casting directors.

*It can also be a chance to appear in an exciting new play, or an established one where you get to play one of your dream roles.

*The venues can be excitingly raw and radical (such as an open-air meat market, a stately home, a public park etc) or high-profile places such as the Edinburgh Festival.

*It's a legitimate way to fill the CV, demonstrating your commitment to theatre at all costs whilst being pro-active.

*It may be a joyous outlet for working with equally frustrated friends.

*The rehearsal schedule and location might enable you to balance it with a day job or be close enough to incur minimal costs.

The Cons (No pun intended):

*The issue of trust - e.g. if no clear understanding is given by a producer as to when the production reaches enough profit, how will the actor know if or when they begin being reimbursed? We are usually the last in the chain to be paid.

*The actor being left severely out of pocket financially if the above factor or poor box office takings do not cover their expenses.

*Disappointing or non-attendance by important industry professionals (if that was the major reason the actor took the risk of this production)

*Incompetence: Not all theatre people are 'equipped' for professional mainstream theatre! What do you know of your director/fellow actors/backstage staff?

*Profit-share theatre is a sensitive and controversial area not just for the above points. Many actors resent the idea of being tempted and manipulated into effectively working for what could be zero reward apart from the play experience. Many of us spend years and a small fortune investing in training to become professional actors, so why should we give our services for nothing, except to charity? After all, this isn't asked of other professionals who are struggling to earn a living. A builder isn't going to painstakingly construct a property for nothing on the off-chance that a client may see it and offer them paid work! The argument that it devalues our credibility is a strong one. So is the counter-argument that our profession is notoriously overcrowded and accepting work like this is more potentially positive than inaction. Ultimately, it's always your choice, not an obligation. Approach it fully-informed and you'll have a more positive and realistic experience.

Weigh up both sides. If you really want to do it and can accept the worst case scenario, then go ahead.

No-Budget/Deferred Payment Film

The world of no-budget and deferred-payment independent film is very much like profit-share theatre. The job is undertaken with no guarantee of payment. In many cases, the most you can expect point-blank is your expenses and sometimes even that isn't given.

There are advantages to the short or feature-length independent film over a theatre piece. For one thing, it's preserved for ever and viewable at one's convenience. Assuming you can get a copy of the film from the company (a common gripe amongst actors - film-makers please note!), it's not limited to a short temporary 'live' run after which it can't be seen again. Even if the actor received no financial recompense for it, they at least have something to show for it as a show-reel or promotional clip on a website. Industry professionals may then be able to see it hopefully when it benefits them and you.

There are also the other showcase possibilities. Firstly, the potential for festival showings, (there are an increasing number of short film festivals) and even the very slim chance of the film being sold to a TV channel or, in the case of a feature, being picked up for theatrical distribution. Likewise, the actor is also showcasing himself to a director or producer of the actual film who may one day emerge as a major player. Yes, that scruffy, uncertain bumfluff-bearded man-boy circling you could be the next Ridley Scott!

Before you project yourself forward into that paparazzi-filled promenade down the strip at Cannes, let's address an area of film work that needs caution in your approach:

Deferred Payment

This is where the artist agrees to 'defer' or postpone their payment for the project till a later time (i.e. when the film is judged by its producers to have gone into profit). Clearly this is as open to exploitation as profit-share theatre and often with more money at stake, since the actor may have committed a long period of expenses and there are many lucrative avenues where they are entitled to their fair share of reward (theatrical release, DVD sales, TV sales etc)

This kind of work is *only to be undertaken if the actor's entitlements are protected in the contract (so let your agent see it) and if you are financially and emotionally prepared to accept zero cash for all your work.*

Even a bona-fide contract is only a mutual agreement as to what you can legally expect. It doesn't mean you will be guaranteed to get it. There are plenty of cases, even on the larger Hollywood scale, where a film has grossed a sizeable revenue but has been 'proven' by creative accounting not to have actually made any profit. If the risks outweigh the gain, stay away; if you can afford the time and expense and would enjoy the project regardless, then commit to it.

CHAPTER 2
TRAINING

One area of great anxiety for beginner actors is the idea of drama training and schools. This chapter is not a critical review of individually named schools since their philosophies change to reflect movement in society and the arts. What I'll discuss here is a realistic assessment of what training should be used for and what to expect from the experience.

To train or not to train

This is a very emotive question, and was a grenade thrown into the field in recent years by David Mamet's superb book *True and False* (see the 'Inspiration' section). Mamet argues that training is unnecessary and harmful. For him there is no substitute for learning by actually doing the work, and that training creates scholars who study rather than actors who fulfil the verb 'to act'. Having spent three years in a structured and very practical drama school system, I feel his criticism is valid – but only of bad schools and unwise choices.

Those who want an academic education in drama will seek that alone and then use it for teaching. Those who start out as actors and then opt for teaching usually reveal their true preference after a while. They find that once confronted with the rigours of what is expected of an actor, they decide it is not for them. (This weeding-out in itself is a good argument for undergoing drama training). Actors who prefer the hands-on learning for a practical career will go to where they know this is clearly offered. If they make a mistake in their school, or the school feels the student is unsuited, the two part company.

It's a sweeping and misleading generalization that somehow formal training robs the actor of their raw creativity and spontaneity. I believe it guides that talent and gives it a mature base to spring from for use anywhere and any time. Many of the seemingly untutored, unpredictable firebrands that inspire us have been formally trained, (Brando, De Niro, Dean etc).

In my opinion, actors whose gifts shrink under the light of study can't have started out with much to begin with. Moreover, if they don't learn to hone their talents they won't respect them or develop the means (or that misunderstood word 'technique') of being able to repeat internal and external expression. They will just trust to the moment if they feel like it. These artists will be later prone to spiral into instability, and flame out from a lack of discipline in their lives. Another way of looking at it is to argue if talent is a bullet, would a professional put it into any shabby old firearm and hope for the best or an instrument that they maintain well and understand?

I agree it would be welcome if there were more opportunities, as in former times, to train by joining a company and learning by doing 'from the ground up'. Sadly the Repertory system that nurtured many older actors is all but dead. So where do the young hopefuls go for good guidance? To simply attach oneself to any company nowadays for tuition runs the risk of placing yourself in the hands of the misguided and untalented. A good drama course for the professional actor is possible; one that is almost totally geared to the practical aspects of 'the doing'. You can learn the craft of respect and interpretation of the text, the technical aspects of the trade and, most neglected of all, some help with negotiating the minefield of business.

I always appreciated my drama school's philosophy (in the period I was there) that encouraged the student to make plenty of mistakes in a safe environment at no cost to anyone's career or production budget. Specifically, this was in terms of being cast against type, stretching my range and comfort zone. I used to be heavily into playing idealists - heroic and fairly bland types without much shading. I was challenged to dig deeper into those ugly, manipulative, unstable and humorous inner elements that did my confidence and self-understanding a power of good. Even when I was utterly miscast or wrong-headed in my approach, it was exhilarating to grow in a controlled hothouse first before being unleashed into the business. I learned more from conflict and arguing my ground than I would have from being poured into a factory line of easy cookie-cutter parts I could have played competently but dully without the training.

How do I choose which school?

This is a key question. Don't rush the decision or base your choice on simply which establishment might accept you. To begin with, for the content side consider the previous chapter's pointers about types of work.

You may not necessarily be able to afford a full-time course of years, but nevertheless it comes down to looking through prospectuses and reports by reliable former and current students. Bear your sources in mind. When basing a judgement on the published memoirs of an actor from some time ago, don't forget there have very likely been some marked changes of staff and philosophy since their era. Equally, contemporaries of yours can be prey to personal grievance and preferences. Get to know the school's current philosophy and get several different recent references.

What kind of training do you want? Ideally, you don't just want to go wherever they will accept you like a parcel in transit. You may not want a Stanislavski-based teaching, or you might feel that's the only method that will satisfy you. Since drama training is a great investment of time and money, aim for the most suitable that will inspire you rather than put you off a later career.

What should I prepare for the audition?

Typically, drama schools ask for two contrasting speeches, a song and the willingness to be flexible if a workshop featuring improvisation is mentioned.

Choosing speeches needs careful and deliberate attention, because it's probably the first time you're confronted with the idea of 'Who am I?" and "What am I displaying of myself in my range and choices?" It's also necessary to have an understanding of 'period' as we're not just in need of a contrast of types but between classical and modern. (There are other aspects to contrast too, as you'll see below)

The best advice I can offer from doing successful auditions and seeing great choices made by others is this:

Lead with a speech that reflects how you come across on a first impression.

This gives your presentation a strong start by showing you understand your apparent appearance and cast-ability and can knowingly play to an audience's expectation.

Let's say you're a wiry, energetic and street-wise looking guy. Look at pieces that could reflect that: classical roles like Edmund in *King Lear*; even Puck in *A Midsummer Night's Dream.* There are great modern choices too – consider that just because the part fits an audience's immediate perception of you, where you take that part from can be a surprise. One of my drama school classmates did a superbly acrobatic and spontaneous Puck that showed character choices so appealing you wanted to play him yourself.

Don't just go for the obvious well-worn ones either. Put out feelers to source the hot new plays around. You can even use prose. I know of one famous actor who dramatised a carriage scene from Dickens' 'Pickwick Papers', playing a multitude of characters.

For the second speech, aim for a contrasting choice the auditioners would not expect from you, but one you know you play well.

Obviously this is harder and yet the most rewarding. A wise selection may make all the difference in impressing the panel. Demonstrating risk and pulling it off would make someone memorable to you, wouldn't it? The same applies to those assessing you.

How do I choose such a contrast? Well, think of the first part you chose and look at opposite qualities to stimulate your ideas. There are many ways you can contrast your two characters.

Comic versus serious *(this is a must.*

Explosive energy versus contemplative reflection

Classical versus modern *(This is a must)*

Low status (weak, frightened) versus high status (arrogant, bullying)

Working class versus high-born

NOTE: The only contrast I would advise you not to attempt is 'age'.

One big mistake an amateur mind brings to auditions is to wheel out a crusty/lovable old character part, when the actor is much too young. This smacks of 'favourite am-dram turn' and is of no help to a school focusing generally on developing the younger model of future actor. It confuses them, wastes their time and if you were convincing could lead to 'See you in twenty years' responses! Even if you're an older Post-Graduate student, stick to your actual age range. For the young auditionee, there are plenty of great parts that could conceivably be in the twenties range.

In my audition for my school many years ago, I had to do three speeches. I led with Odysseus from *The Odyssey* from a full-length play I had toured with my Youth Theatre and Shylock from *The Merchant Of Venice* (not the best idea – see above, but I had played the part already and attempted to age him down somewhat). These varied in status and tone but in my naivety would not have been varied enough to get me in. However, my magic bullet was my third selection. Arnold from *Torch Song Trilogy* is a gay New York drag queen whose waspish playful wit, paranoia and touching hopefulness were a world away from the other men's masculine old-world values, humourlessness and resolve. Arnold's accent was also a firm contrast to the standard R.P. of Odysseus and the clipped, guttural sound I used for Shylock (a peculiar variation of South-African). He was great fun to play and I relished slipping on his silk dressing gown in my mind and playing seductively with the onlookers. I believe this was what got me through the door.

How do I handle rejection?

To be hit with rejection before you even begin training as an actor is harsh. You haven't yet built the armour of resolve to let it wash over you and carry on. How much notice should you take of it at this stage? Just because they've rejected me, does it mean I shouldn't try again? Well, if they offer you any detailed criticism, it may be worth giving an ear. If they simply say no, well you can't draw anything helpful from that so move along and seek another outlet for your development.

It all depends on what you're told. A good friend of mine was once condemned at a drama school audition as 'Too fat to be an actor'. Being overweight is a note of concern for your health, but the credibility of an outright dismissal just on that basis is blasted out of the water when you think of the myriad great character players on the well-fed side, (Charles Laughton, Brian Blessed, John Candy etc). Fortunately he dismissed their criticism and took his place with me at my school where I was much the happier for his company.

You may be told specific pointers to work on that are encouraging. A panel may feel you lack a clear reason why you want to be an actor, or that you seem too inexperienced in life just yet to have the creative pool to draw from. Neither of course is a value judgement about your talent, so they are elements to work on quite easily if you accept them

When it's your talent that is being denigrated, this is where you must dig deep and truly listen to what your heart tells you. Yes, tenacity can overcome weaknesses, and learned skills can make up for raw burning talent, yet you must connect with what is really at the core of your need in life. I can't tell you whether this business is the right one for you. There are as many untalented delusionals clogging up the industry as there are worthwhile strugglers. The point is to return to the trust in your own opinion. Know when to be unstoppably focused and when to back down. Truly having ultimate faith in yourself is a quality that will be tested time and again. Can you handle that? Be honest. It may save you a lot of anguish down the wrong road.

What can I expect from the teaching?

Hopefully, you'll gain some good tools for character work and a better appreciation and experience of different text styles and periods than you would elsewhere. I'd like to think you will also get a microcosm of what the profession is really like on the outside, the good and the bad. By this I mean students who are lazy and disrespectful, (and I trust they will be bounced out to make way for those who want to be there). I want you to have the wonderful sense of camaraderie and team spirit possible in a creative environment. I also hope you get some excellent directors and one or two who are flawed: egotistical and tyrannical, prone to favouritism or just incompetent. Not often, but just enough to allow you to appreciate what makes a good one.

You may also get the offer of some good extra classes in skills such as dance forms, physical theatre, even acrobatics.

Take advantage of them; you never know when you might want them later. It's not like algebra in your early school days. If I had a pound for every time an actor pined: "I wish I'd paid attention in such-and-such a class…"

Valuable drama training is also a reality check. It should benefit the whole profession, nurturing the real talent, tactfully disabusing the desperate untalented 'wannabee' and culling the timewasters.

Looking back

Probably the most profound thing I wish I could have known about drama school training before I did it was that it is the beginning not the end of your study. It passes by like a sprint, with ambitious people jostling for parts and places, yet the profession outside is actually a marathon. When you're out in the business, that's where the more mature test of your commitment and character takes place. You may be favoured in your training with great parts, overlooked and disheartened, or both if you're fortunate, as I was. Once you leave the safe spoon-fed nest of given parts and have to go and seek your fortune on your own, that's where you sharpen your tools and ultimately prove your worth to the only director that matters: YOU.

In a union survey, it was found that a staggering 95% of drama graduates leave the business within five years of graduation. Which side will you be on?

CHAPTER 3
MIND, BODY
AND SPIRIT

In this section are powerful options for optimum health for the mental, physical and touching on the spiritual side - all the elements that integrate in the life of the actor. All three parts need separate care, but all function in perfect inner harmony. They combine even more potently when you determine a strong vision to unite them.

I'll begin with the workshop of the mind, where our dreams and goals are crystallised and activated. Then we go to the body, the engine that carries the precious cargo along its designated path.

Connecting with spirit beyond the day-to-day bodily concerns allows us to check that what we ask for is in harmony with our nature and those around us. It's impossible to achieve any personal desire if deep down it conflicts with other sincere beliefs you have, such as wishing for wealth but knowing you would feel guilty about having it when someone else doesn't. Many people have no particular spiritual or religious beliefs. They may choose to disregard any references I make beyond the physical. I however believe spirituality also aids the fulfilment of desire by working along unseen channels while the conscious mind is busily doing the hands-on work.

Training your Mental and Emotional Focus

"We become what we think about all day long"
(Ralph Waldo Emerson)

Since the wise actor is a constant student of human beings, we all benefit from understanding and developing ourselves too. We are fortunate enough to be working in an art form where we get to wield a hammer in the white-hot furnace of human emotions. Only the stable, centred performer should be in charge of such volatile substances! Only by being in command of our own passions and destiny to begin with, can we enjoy the emotional rollercoaster of the business (and be equipped to play those characteristics of another person) without losing our sanity or quitting in disillusionment.

Let's deal with a few mental and emotional blocks and then put theory into practice by releasing your goals: how to state them, have faith in them and make them happen.

The myth

The most damaging misconception we have about our thoughts and emotions as humans is that we are victims of them not in charge of them.

"Sometimes I'm in a bad mood or I feel depressed - we all do. It just happens. So what? "

It's amazing how little responsibility people take for what they believe and how they behave. I'm not telling you anything you don't already know. I'll bet even if you agree with those statements above, you've experienced yourself or others saying variations of these:

"It was Sarah's birthday. I couldn't avoid drinking. That's why I was late and hung over in rehearsal"

"The director looked really bored. That's why I didn't give a good audition. He didn't like me"

"I would have performed better if the bus hadn't made me late"

The list goes on and so do the excuses.

We secretly know who the real saboteur is, but we will fight like alley cats to avoid taking responsibility. Why don't we own up? There are three compelling reasons:

a) It's easier to put the blame elsewhere than admit we are in charge.

b) We gain a reward from the behaviour that keeps us repeating it.

c) Not fully understanding what responsibility means.

The truth

1) You are responsible for EVERYTHING you think and feel.

2) You are ultimately responsible for EVERYTHING you do.

Read those statements a few times. Question them. Think of situations from your past. Do you feel some resistance now? Maybe you've thought of exceptions, times where:

"I wasn't responsible for that! That wasn't my fault"

Now try this:

3) Responsibility is not the same as *blame.*

Part of the reason for not accepting enough responsibility is that we misunderstand what the term really means:

Response–ability: Our ability to be accountable for how we choose to react to a situation we are in or have experienced before. It doesn't mean we are necessarily the one who caused it – but we are accountable for *how we react as a result of it.*

I wouldn't dream of over-simplifying awful traumas like childhood abuse or adult domestic violence. We cannot possibly be to blame for such things being forced upon us, especially in the great vulnerability of youth. Where we can take control and be accountable is in choosing to liberate ourselves from replaying painful events repeatedly *as though they are still happening to us* and preventing us from moving past them into fulfilment personally and professionally. When we make ourselves relive past traumas and blocks, it isn't the event or the actual culprit that is still causing the pain: it is us. Every day if unchecked we can victimise ourselves and others in much more subtle ways: "How do you expect me to behave, after what my childhood was like?" may inspire compassion when a relationship breaks down again, but won't get you very far when you're late and disorganised three times in a row for your theatre company meetings!

When will you take responsibility for who you are *now?*

With your acting, you may not have got very far up to today. Is it just bad luck? Not having the breaks or influence of other people to assist you? Or is it possible you are involved, an accessory even in the hampering of your own progress? It's surprising how when we dig deep enough, if we get beyond the initial strenuous denials we find that part of the limitation may be self-imposed. Instead of regarding acting success as being an exclusive party to which we're not invited, it's as likely to be one where we all have a password, but you've temporarily forgotten it.

"That's all very well, but with only a finite number of jobs we can't all be in work at any one time", they cry. That doesn't stop you going out and generating your own productions.

There's a positive response to every imagined setback you throw in front of yourself – and it should always put a challenge squarely where it belongs:

How are YOU going to change it?

Since we choose all our voluntary responses to situations, we are much more in charge of our careers as actors than we think. Remove the psychology that has you believing you are a powerless employee waiting to be discovered. Think like that and you will always feel like a humble victim and 'get what you're given'. Kenneth Branagh's frustration at what he saw as a future of typecasting in policeman roles propelled him into doing a one–man show and forming his own company, playing the parts he wanted on his terms.

Now I'm not suggesting everyone should aim to become an actor-manager. What is important though is having a vision for your career that revolves around being active and more responsible for how the industry sees you. You may be happy with the narrow view casting directors have of you, and of your status playing the waiting game of the hired hand. If you aren't, then do the things that teach people to perceive you how you want to be seen. Mount your own show or pioneer your own film and invite the influential to see it. There are many ways you can have more influence in your own destiny. (Consider the opportunities in the Showcase section of the Agents chapter)

When you honestly begin to own what you believe, and the events you're always co-conspiring to happen, a subtle and profound shift happens. You go from being an ineffectual supporting player to being the centre-stage power in what happens to you. More welcome trust will be given to you, and people in your life begin to treat you in a different way. Those who until now thought they could manipulate you to fit their agenda will think twice.

People's opinions of us are surprisingly open to influence when they are presented with a convincing enough counter-argument. They may be initially unwilling to change their agenda but will eventually share the truthful perception of you that you want - *when you show it to them.*

You will soon have the pleasure of feeling less volatile generally, less quick to revert to the impotent anger of "Why me?" as a reaction to circumstances. This is because you recognise you were the one allowing yourself to be upset and can just as emativeeringly take charge in doing something about it.

At the same time that you begin to see you are accountable for your behaviour, you also see where other people are responsible for *their* behaviour. It's a question of knowing the balance. Here's an example from my own professional life:

I once came out of a TV audition where on the drive home I kept swinging between anger and trying to pacify myself. The anger was getting the better of my normally even temperament and would not lie low. I'd performed unusually poorly, continually forgetting the tiniest number of lines I have ever had in a script. Now the director, on greeting me in the room, spent the first two minutes of our meeting texting someone on her mobile, which left me sitting in a rude uncomfortable silence. She then made no effort to describe the piece, treating the whole process with barely disguised boredom before hearing me deliver my lines so haphazardly it stunned me. I left shell-shocked at how amateurish I had been and livid at her rudeness.

On reflection, I realised that despite her responsibility for very poor manners in treating an auditionee, my bursts of anger were really aimed within. I was ashamed of having allowed her manner to affect me, but more so for exposing my complacency in the blasé way I had learned the lines, thinking I could give such a tiny part with little preparation. Had I treated the script with more respect, she could have been as frosty as an ice-pop and I would still have delivered the goods on camera. I was ultimately responsible for that result and no-one else. Once I admitted this to myself, bingo! The rage vanished and the awful tension I'd manifested in my body began to dissolve. I had reclaimed the power I lost.

The freedom

When you get beyond the stubborn refusal and passing of the buck to accept you are totally responsible for the course of your life and career, it's a very liberating new feeling. Instead of anticipating unwanted extra pressure and work, (a very powerful incentive not to have tried this before), you can now feel so much more hopeful and capable. The strength within you can now be applied with a far greater confidence and purpose to creating, not destroying. In other words, you can put things right with just as much conviction as you made them wrong.

How the mind assists

The mind is like the immensely powerful genie of the fairy tale. It continually grants us whatever we focus on and even works for us in our sleep. Here's a quick illustration you may have taken for granted: How it is that you can set an alarm clock for a particular time and frequently you wake up just before it wakes you? Because without even being conscious of it, you instructed your mind what time you wanted to be awake...*and it obeyed you without any external influence.*

Like any great power, it comes with great responsibility though, because it gives us:

EVERYTHING WE WANT and

EVERYTHING WE DON'T WANT.

We must be diligent then to ensure that the negative possibilities and events in life are only given as much attention as it takes to avert them. Instead, our concentration is best devoted to emphasising what we positively want to happen.

Let's look then, at the 'magical' results of harnessing positive intent...

What the decision attracts

The Latin root of 'decide' means 'to cut off from all alternatives'. This is precisely what the actor must do in order to state one's dream and hold fast to it. Many actors' dreams take an extraordinary amount of dedication, so the greater the clarity and resolve, the greater the results.

The good news is that when you decide to only give valuable attention to what you want, nature begins to pull strings to help you:

'The Law of Attractive Attraction' states that once you make a firm commitment to a goal, the outcome will come to you as speedily as you move toward it. Your proposed destiny moves from being a single idea to a partnership between you and the cosmos.

Secondly, for those who prefer hard science to the spiritual element for evidence, there is actually a part of the brain called the Reticular Activating Cortex which comes into play when a clear goal is stated. It brings to our attention images and opportunities in the outside world that relate to what we have decided so we can use them. For example, have you ever wanted a particular car and then found that suddenly you're so much more aware of that model of car on the roads? There's nothing spooky about it. Your reality has simply been changed by your internal 'programming' to be heightened to images on the outside that reflect your conscious thoughts.

This also works disastrously to keep manifesting the very thing you want *not* to happen, as in 'Be careful what you wish for – you may just get it'. Isn't it uncanny how often bad news habitually happens to people you know who always dwell on that possibility?

The mind makes no protective distinction between what will harm or benefit you when you dwell on things - so focus on what you actually want.

When you work with enough desire and a sound enough plan for achieving it, eventually the plan itself somehow gets in the driver's seat and takes unstoppable command of you till you get to your destination. That's when you know you're doing what you were meant to.

Why have goals?

The incredibly potent tool of your mind works whether you are awake or asleep, always sifting through ideas, considering options and guiding you to some form of fulfilment. It's never dormant so be warned - unless you occupy it consciously with your desires based on your values, someone else will be only too willing to have you operate according to *their* agenda!

The more benign reason for being goal-oriented is that I firmly believe we humans are designed to follow purpose during our lives. It's what we are supposed to do. It brings out the best in us, gives us compelling reasons for getting up every morning rather than just existing or coping. When a fellow actor (or indeed anyone) tells me they are dispirited, rootless, downhearted or just plain frustrated about their lives, what they are responding to is not that life itself is meaningless but: 'I've lost the reason for showing up'. They no longer have a clear purpose to be inspired by and the confidence from results to keep them enthused and in the game. When we cut ourselves off from clear purpose, we lose the juice that energises and powers who we are. Having energy is the direct result of how much we care about doing something. Certainly drugs can valuably mask messages of pain, but they also mute the messages to the spirit that say "Find a good purpose".

Since we now appreciate how sensitive our consciousness is to granting us whatever we dwell on, and how important that direction is to our wellbeing, isn't this the perfect time to actually set out our goals?

This is the exciting part: **The vision**

Find a place and time where you are undisturbed for a while. Have some sheets of paper and a pen with you. Settle somewhere quietly where you can sit or lie comfortably. Switch off that mobile. Remove all outer distractions.

Close your eyes. Take a few deep breaths. Centre yourself. You're about to connect with the deepest, most private part of yourself...

Now, do you remember the moment when you first made up your mind "I want to be an actor"? For some, it may be further back to recapture than others. Maybe one time you were seeing a particular film or a stage production. Perhaps you had an experience that was beyond words, where your resolve deep down just seemed to turn over like a mighty boulder and fall squarely into place as if to say "That's it. That is what I want to do".

For me it was performing in a Tom Stoppard play at school when I was fifteen. I thought I wanted to be a writer until I felt the audience's attention and heard the laughter and approval coming from them. The immediacy of that reaction was intoxicating and I knew then that to be an actor was the most thrillingly alive thing I could do.

I want you to regain that rush, that certainty – however it came to you.

It is vital that whatever we wish for, we fill it with our desire; 'emotionalise' it as Napoleon Hill says in *Think and Grow Rich*. It's not enough to have an intellectual understanding of our aim, a dry idea that it would make sense to do this somehow. This is not a thesis we're writing for a college course. This is the awakening of our heart's desire to propel us forward, to pull us toward it, and only something we have a burning desire to express will stay glowing like a burning ember in the snow when things get tough. It is beyond reason; it is the core of you that must be satisfied no matter what obstacles may come.

Feel it now. Feel it build. Hear the noises around you. Remember what you saw that filled you with sensations you had to have again.

Take that excitement and bring it here into the present.

How does it feel?

How strong is the passion?

Now…what do you want in your life from this point onward?

What do you see yourself creating in the future?

Have it all – no holds barred – brainstorm every idea, every wish. Every creative idea and experience is permitted here.

Allow images and feelings to flash across your consciousness like an exciting, appetising sexy trailer for your forthcoming life. This is a film of your future – and the wonderful thing is, you are going to go beyond being a passive observer. You get to live it!

What kind of parts are they? Romantic? Tragic? Swash-buckling? Gritty? Slapstick hilarity?

Where do you see yourself? How specific can you be?

On stage…where?

On the cinema screen?

On a hit television sitcom watched by helplessly laughing millions?

In a school or community venue, connecting with young audiences, feeling their delight and involvement?

Your creativity is limitless. Have you always wanted to play a musical instrument? To paint? Dance?

Have it all.

As the images grow more and more vivid, *now project yourself into the pictures.* Inhabit the costumes, feel the lights, see the film crew gathered around you as 'Action' is called and all eyes are on you to give them the magic.

Make these images as bright and as detailed as you can. They are the source of your dreams and will form the bedrock of the plans you are about to make…

Now take a piece of paper. We're going to get this down while it's fresh and alive. For the next ten minutes, I'd like you to download from your memory every image you saw of yourself in that future. Be detailed with each one. If you were in a particular venue, or playing a definite part, record it. Let your imagination add to them. The visions you had before are the catalyst. As you experience each one, others may come to mind – capture them. Censor nothing. Flex your creative muscles. If an image isn't quite clear, note what is vivid about it and move on. This is a time for bottling lightning, not dwelling. We'll make sense of it all afterwards.

Now finish the list.

How did that feel? Was it liberating, and possibly a little overwhelming? It's not often enough adults allow ourselves free rein to daydream. It's a highly under-rated practise that has fuelled the invention of anything truly worthwhile in the world.

Incidentally, allow yourself to feel another emotion at this point: *pride.* Did you know you've just put yourself into the top 5% of achievers? That's how few people ever sit down and commit to paper what they truly want out of life. Even if you take a wish list like this and deposit it unused in a desk drawer, its power already goes to work for you, simply because you stated it to the world.

The detail

Look at the list. Hopefully you can decipher that high-speed scrawl because now I invite you to give shape and order to bring your fantasy a step closer to reality. Yes, even unbridled creativity needs a little discipline.

I'll bet as you go down the list its fulfilment looks pretty daunting. "I only have one life! How am I going to manage all this, find time for a love life and pay the gas bill?" Hold your horses. Before resistance creeps in, understand that you're seeing the whole thing in one big picture. This is the overview - of course it's going to look monumental. Did I say you were expected to achieve it all at once? If I itemised everything you did last year and presented you with it on January 1, you'd wonder how on earth you found the time and energy for all that. With some intelligent organisation, your results can be (pardon the pun) dramatic.

The key is to divide the picture into manageable sections. Look at the list again, and notice this time that each desire will take a varying amount of time to achieve. Some may take years, while others could be done within one year or less. (Starting singing lessons is only be a phone call away).

Now you have the means of organising your plan of attack take five sheets of paper. It's time for the serious part of the fun. Write a heading for each one according to One Year, Three Years, Five Years, Ten Years and Twenty Years from today, (well when's a better day to begin the rest of your life?).

Be specific by naming the exact date ahead of today for each page.

For example, if today is March 12th, then for the One Year page, put March 12th followed by the year number following this year. This sends a firmer, more specific instruction to your mind than a general 'One Year' statement. You are committing to an actual date of fulfilment ahead of you. The mind is highly suggestible as we said earlier, so tell it precisely what you want to do.

Now go through your list and decide which goals are feasible within One Year and beyond and share them out

Priorities

Aim for an even spread so no single page is overloaded. If you find you're overburdening your first year for example, weigh up 'What is most important to me within the time frame?' Is getting a new agent crucial for me this year or can that wait?

Set realistic targets that make you reach but not exceed your capabilities. Too often, goals such as New Year resolutions are sabotaged by unworkable targets which then collapse in defeat. Goal-setting is a delicate balancing act, an investment in inspiring a series of gradual increasing results.

Motivation works in two stages:

1) The desire *at the beginning* for generating exciting results.

2) A continually renewing confidence *as each stage is completed.*

You'll probably find that the further you project into future pages, the more general and simply defined some goals become. That's perfectly fine. Many of the details in some goals may be found later in the stages leading to its' eventual achievement.

Once you've divided up the list to spread across each period, lay out the pages and survey the field of battle. Congratulations! You've now taken what previously could have been dismissed as pie-in-the-sky fantasies and given a broad strategy to begin to actually take them seriously.

The next step is to focus the laser beam of the mind on to a more detailed plan for actually carrying out your first year.

Goals within goals

Let's get to grips now with your One Year list. I fully expect your goals here to be stated very simply as end results. Starting with the first one, in order to succeed what steps would you need to take to make it happen? Each goal will usually require a series of actions so break it down into sub-stages. When you can measure progress, you can stay motivated. It's more intelligent to take time achieving something in small pieces than trying to take it unrealistically in one hurdle and then giving up.

As an example, let's use the target of getting a new agent. (We'll assume you don't currently have one). You may have written: 'Get an agent'. This is the end result, a clear and simple aim and excellent as a starting point. However, since it can't simply be done in one move you need stages along the way to carry it out. Consider how you might break this down into a sensible plan of action. Be as detailed as you need as long as it contains real progress and flexibility if necessary.

Here's one suggested plan:

*ASK FRIENDS FOR REFERRALS

*USE INTERNET + 'CONTACTS' BOOK

*LIST AGENTS TO APPLY TO

*WRITE/CALL REFERRED AGENTS

*INTERVIEW WITH AGENTS

*PLAN SHOWCASE TO BE SEEN IN (IF ABOVE OPTIONS FAIL)

*MEET COLLEAGUES TO DISCUSS SHOW IDEAS

*FIND AND BOOK VENUE

*PLAN MARKETING AND MAILSHOTS

*SHORTLIST AGENTS + CASTING DIRECTORS

*REHEARSE CHOSEN SHOW

*MAIL/CALL SHORTLIST

*WRITE THANKYOU LETTERS TO MY SHORTLIST AFTER THE SHOW

Waiting for the results is not listed at the end since it doesn't count as active behaviour!

Now the rest is up to you.

The goals can be reduced to however small you need them in order for you to achieve them piece by piece.

A contract with the self

Some time ago, when I first read Napoleon Hill's remarkable *Think and Grow Rich*, (a must-have for anyone's library) I was impressed by the section where he invites the reader to write out a contract. Unlike any other, this is a contract with oneself. It's a beautiful concept because it's a private contract that you alone will sign. It has only one side that needs to uphold its end of the bargain: yours. Essentially this works as a written and dated agreement that in return for providing you with the fulfilment of very specific goals by the date you set, you agree to commit whatever time and labour is needed to make it happen. I wholeheartedly recommend writing one out, summing up the most important crystallised life desires you have and the date by which you want them to materialise in your life.

Take time to consider the content and read it aloud to yourself every day – with feeling. Etch the commitment to it in your feelings. It's a tremendous way of encapsulating the goals you wrote about in such detail above, and will help to keep you on track.

Nowadays, individuals and even companies produce 'Mission Statements' – the same principle applies except this is a statement of continual purpose to clarify objectives and keep its owner focused on service. I mention this because as I was finishing the first draft of this chapter, I found one by chance, written by someone I admire very much: Bruce Lee.

I was aware that Lee absorbed a lot of personal development texts as part of his disciplines during his tragically short life, including the work of Napoleon Hill. What I didn't know till now was that he penned a mission statement in 1969 outlining his aims for an explosively successful career as the foremost martial arts actor in America – *two years before* his first movie crossed the Atlantic and began making his name:

"I, Bruce Lee, will be the first highest paid Oriental superstar in the United States. In return, I will give the most exciting performances and render the best of quality in the capacity of an actor. Starting 1970 I will achieve world fame and from then onward till the end of 1980 I will have in my possession $10,000,000. I will live the way I please and achieve inner harmony and happiness."

The sheer certainty with which he stakes his claim and the fact that he then made it come true so gloriously means a lot to me. It perfectly embodies the principle of stating your desires clearly and agreeing to render the fullest service possible. Sadly of course the latter half of his statement could not come to fruition, but then the future as they say is promised to none of us. How bright his flame burned in the time he had though. And the short life he did live unfolded as he wanted it – by his design.

Recommended materials:

Books:

Think and Grow Rich - Napoleon Hill

(Original version – the updated versions sacrifice valuable chapters)

Your Erroneous Zones – Dr Wayne Dyer

(Time Warner - 2005)

Manifesto – Barefoot Doctor

(Element Books - 2005)

CDs:

How To Be A No-Limit Person – Dr Wayne Dyer

(Nightingale Conant - 4 CDs)

The Weekend Seminar - Jim Rohn

(12 CDs – www.jimrohn.com)

Being in flow

The steps in your list of goals are an involved process; so is a shopping list for the supermarket and how intimidating is that to perform? A plan of goals when you undertake them is like a boulder you begin to roll. Once the energy for the groundwork of the goals has been invested, the boulder's movement soon becomes a sequence in flow where all you then do is 'top up' the momentum as you move it along. You've mapped out a plan whose details the mind can consciously and unconsciously begin to work on. (Did I say congratulations by the way?)

There is no force, no pressure; banish such negative associations from your mind. After all, you looked within yourself and ensured that the desires you visualise are absolutely in harmony with who you are and what you feel will fulfil your own true mission here. This is simply acting on purpose, so if it's in harmony it takes no more energy for its fulfilment than it really needs.

In Taoism, they call this 'Wu Wei'- action through inaction. It doesn't mean you literally do nothing, yet it may feel wonderfully like this. Behaving in alignment with your true self can seem effortless, tapping into a rich seam of additional energy that tells you you're on the right path. (That's what I feel as I'm writing this book!).

Physical Health

Your health is the best investment you can make in your life. When most of us think of an investment in life we think of money. We can see it, touch it, watch it grow and spend it on tangible things. However, if you don't have good physical, mental, spiritual and emotional health, you can't earn money and you can't properly enjoy spending it. In fact, you will not be able to truly enjoy anything in life.

Here I want to touch on the opportunities you have to invest in your physical health, and far from being a chore it's a fantastic springboard to enable you to turbo-charge your body, mind and outlook on life.

Its remarkable how often people pay lip service to health until they become ill. They talk about its importance, yet when it comes to either paying a gym membership or taking the time for doing their own exercise at home, their other perceived priorities quickly shout it down:

"I haven't got time to go running / work out at home…"

"Gym membership is too expensive…"

"I'll do it next week / in the new year…"

If you give most people a pie chart to divide up, illustrating the relative importance of the different elements of their life (partner, children, family, health, financial security, recreation, social life etc), generally when presented with this diagram they may include health as a fairly generous slice of the pie. It seems important there in that whole life picture and makes inarguable sense.

If you then provide a second chart asking that same person to depict honestly what percentage of their resources are *actually* spent on health, the reality of its lack of importance is glaringly obvious. It's hardly worth picking up the knife for that slice!

Consider these two truisms:

"If you think training is expensive, try ignorance"

"If you can't make time for health, you'd better make time for illness"

Weeks of valuable time are being lost each year to illnesses brought on by lifestyle choices that are avoidable. For the majority of the public, good health is vital. For the actor, investing in *superior* mental and physical health is crucial. Just being without illness or infection is not enough. The actor's body and mind receive profound tests every day at a higher than average pitch and the instrument has to be prepared each day instead of trying to cope and react afterward.

In your career, you will need a highly developed body to handle more expressive physical rigours than most jobs. You will also need greater mental and emotional discipline than most people as you experience a wider and deeper spectrum of emotions both in and away from performance than normal life demands.

The body and mind are one entity. The actor who wants to be any good at their craft knows they can only express a character fully when they can access their body, mind, emotions and voice altogether whenever they need and at whatever heightened level they want to call on.

The discipline

Discipline is one of those words that conjure up an image of po-faced severe cruelty. Instead, think of the discipline of health as much more encouraging and positive: investing in the future.

'The readiness is all' as Shakespeare wrote. How much easier it is to get into the swing of early calls, daily exercise warm-ups and physical vigour in rehearsal and performance when your body/mind is already attuned to be that responsive. An unaccustomed soul dragged out of bed and into a day of demands is resisting not embracing what the work brings. An actor who is ready and has been preparing for this project is like a coiled spring of charged anticipation, not a slug-a-bed. They know they are ready and have been planning for it even before the job appeared.

Not only is the disciplined health-conscious actor better equipped, they deserve it more – and that noticeable readiness may have actually got them the job in the first place. No one can fairly expect a director to imagine a vibrant, fit confident actor unless there is one in front of them. As with the vivid creation of a character, you stand a much better chance if you don't force the decision-maker to have to work to see it.

I believe there is also a spiritual element to regular body/mind discipline for the actor. The dream career opportunities of a performer who wills themselves each day to make ready, even in barren periods, is actually bringing those dreams a step closer. They are consciously aligning their inner and outer world to match the success they want beyond today. He or she is becoming a stronger, more resilient, unstoppable self-respecting human being - *and that's the kind of person to whom great opportunities 'seem to happen'.*

The life of the actor is a potential feast of all kinds of bodily temptations on offer. There are the endless opportunities for the commonplace (booze and cigarettes at parties, late night pub socialising after a job or drowning your sorrows because you don't have one) to the more sinister (available drugs at affluent showbiz parties, and adultery!). Many of them come with the added hook of peer pressure. Since your fellow cast members are doing it, not joining in is seen as anti-social. Moderation is always the best tactic. If you're going to be seduced by something that only serves the body, how about choosing something that benefits rather than sabotages?

Exercise

There are far too many actors in the profession whose bodies have run to fat due to poor lifestyle excess. Unless it is due to unavoidable illness, the cause is not necessary. Attempting to get back 'in shape' after years of abuse or neglect can exact a heavy price to pay. The body also doesn't appreciate it if we let it lie untended when we are 'resting' and then suddenly put hefty demands on it for a show

Install the good disciplines while you are young enough if you can. If you're into middle-age or have been recovering from illness, then join your local gym anyway but please take medical advice from your G.P. first and begin *gradually*.

If the gym has a studio, ask about classes. Many people use lack of motivation as an excuse; without a 'gym buddy' to go with, they feel they will slack off till they stop going. Well, you can't rely on a friend to always be there. An alternative is to attend classes which most gym chains and independent ones feature. They cover all tastes and levels and the in-built group motivation pushes you that bit further.

For a gentle stretching workout try Tai Chi, Yoga or Pilates. For cardiovascular sessions where you can break a sweat without going crazy, you might like aerobic, step or a Hip-Hop, Street Dance style class with a lively group 'vibe'.

For the more high-impact workout, there are variations like Boxercise or Combat which incorporate very intense choreographed punches and kicks (solo) to pumping music tracks, and circuit classes that consist of a number of workout stations that you move around one at a time with often no rest between each. Group classes for muscle toning and sculpting are also quite common and again form a necessary part of fitness for areas that are impacted on in performance. The more hard-core of these classes are best left till you're assured of a strong heart and are free of any injuries. Ask the instructors and your G.P.

Discussion about body discipline wouldn't be complete without a slightly more detailed look at a couple of classes that combine physical exertion with spiritual connection and calmness. After all, many believe that we aren't just creatures of the body and mind; that there is the spirit to integrate into the whole.

Yoga

One perfect example of the bridge between the mind and body is the practise of Yoga. Derived from the Sanskrit for 'To join or unite' it is a Hindu discipline aimed at achieving a state of perfect spiritual insight and tranquillity. In the West the term is most commonly understood as the physical exercises that are practiced as part of this discipline.

In a calm and respectful atmosphere you are encouraged to connect with the body, stretch each muscle group and focus inward. It's a superb workout if you spend a lot of time sitting driving, or at a desk, allowing you to balance and align muscle groups that we often misuse through unconsciously bad posture. Yoga is also useful for conditions such as anxiety, arthritis, headache, migraine, multiple sclerosis, osteoporosis, pregnancy, rheumatoid arthritis, and more.

After a good Yoga session, I always gain a clear feeling of peace and centeredness regardless of what state I brought in to the class. There are varying types of yoga and a good instructor in a class will offer beginner and advanced postures for all experience levels.

Tai Chi

Based on ancient Chinese teachings from over 6,000 years ago, Tai Chi combines breath, movement and meditation in slow graceful movements based on original fighting blows. Adapted to a slow stylised manner, it enhances the vital energy flow through the body, improves blood circulation and the body's immune system. When performed correctly, it also brings the muscles, organs and skeletal structure back into proper alignment.

There are excellent spiritual techniques and classes available that can enrich whatever practices you have already in your life. These very much compliment the disciplines of the mind and create a harmonious connection for the body to express in daily life.

Meditation

'All men's miseries derive from not being able to sit in a quiet room alone' (Pascal)

Meditation is widely accepted as a powerful form of alternative medicine, bringing mental calmness and physical relaxation by suspending the stream of insistent and distracting thoughts normally occupying the mind. It reduces stress, alters hormone levels and elevates one's mood. It requires no physical effort and very effectively grounds the body and mind before exertions such as the classes above.

Meditation may be used beyond emptying the mind. Once at peace, your focus can be placed upon a single dominant desire - anything from wishing a sick loved one to be healed to the desire for a particular acting opportunity. The more specific you are the better. A form such as Japa meditation allows the reciting of a mantra during which the goal may be visualised. An excellent example of this is the CD *Meditations for Manifesting* by Wayne Dyer. He explains the principle and practise before delivering sessions suitable for both morning and evening.

The other side benefits for an actor of a regular gym class discipline are that it's very much like continuing the structured training regimen of drama school days. Those that involve choreography are excellent for the part of the brain that even for non-dancing actors may one day be brought into play in a chorus line. The combat-style classes could even serve as a general tuning-up of stage fight capabilities and physical reaction speed.

Gyms are also good for adding to your social life, and as the most popular classes are often in the evenings it's a welcome safe zone to take out frustration from that day job!

There will be days where you may be required to go to a rehearsal or audition very early, so why not install a daily routine of exercises that limber up the body/mind and even the voice so you are 'programmed' for whatever may happen? Psycho-Calisthenics in Patrick Holford's book *Six Weeks To Super Health* are a great physical warm-up. Each exercise stretches the various muscle groups and every movement is informed by the breath, thus also benefiting the actor with increased lung capacity over time.

I'm don't claim to be an expert nutritionist but it's wise to be sensitive to your body's tolerance for alcohol, caffeine and certain types of foods that we may take to excess. Get to know the types of foods that are detrimental, and those that can increase your energy when you need the extra zing!

Recommended materials:

Books:
Six Weeks To Super Health - Patrick Holford
(Piatkus Book – 2002)
Ageless Body, Timeless Mind –Dr Deepak Chopra
(Rider & Co - 2003)
Grow Younger, Live Longer- Dr Deepak Chopra
(Rider & Co - 2002)
There Is A Spiritual Solution To Every Problem
– Dr Wayne Dyer
(HarperCollins - 2002)
The Road Less Travelled -M Scott Peck
(Arrow – 1990)

CDs:
Living Beyond Miracles - Dr Wayne Dyer & Dr Deepak
Chopra
(Amber Allen - 1993)

CHAPTER 4
INSPIRATION

Pursuing our dreams and gradually seeing the progress along our chosen path is a great motivation for keeping us going. We can also enrich that journey with other empowering sources of inspiration – from fellow travellers. I daresay you're already doing this, yet it's surprising how many more opportunities we have for further reinforcing our enthusiasm.

Faith and the actor

Acting attracts many whose nomadic search for work and regular immersion into another soul's experience makes them very receptive to different spiritual ideas. This may be taken too far at times - some showbiz folk seem to be no more than spiritual 'tourists' moving from faith to faith like followers of the hottest exercise craze. I Respect those whose adherence to an established faith gives them a firm foundation against the uncertainty of the actor's life. However, what's true of us all is that on some level we each practise a form of faith:

The assurance of things hoped for / The Conviction of things not seen

(Hebrews 11:1)

If that quotation from the Bible doesn't define our approach to acting as a career, what does? Basically, we have no demonstrable proof that the 'things not seen' which we want for ourselves will turn into any actual success. The odds are supremely against us. We are fully aware it is an immensely overcrowded business. We know the statistics. Our training is nowhere near as likely to lead to a single job as that of a doctor or most other professions. Our talent is also no guarantee since there's plenty of that around in varying degrees. These facts should utterly discourage us - yet they don't. Why? Because the actor who manifests success has *faith* in their ability to achieve it. Their desire and commitment to what they love doing is such that they see it and work for it without having the proof first...except in their heart and mind. They cannot be swayed from their belief.

It is 'unreasonable'. It's beautiful in its simplicity. It's the secret of how all great achievements in the world begin through the act of seeing it materialise in the potential world before it happens in the real world.

At the same time we must never neglect that it has to be backed up with action.

Modelling others

When you think about the kind of career you want, the type of parts and the fellow artists and environment you'd like to work in, are there particular actors who inspire you? Ones who've built a body of work or who are creating a distinct path of success now that you'd like to emulate? I'm not suggesting copying someone else, (we all need to be appreciated for our individuality), but even the most aggressively individual performer is inspired by others who've gone before them.

What I'm talking about is the intelligent and selective use of *'modelling'*. This is a term used in Neuro-Linguistic Programming (NLP) for the conscious study and practise of a highly successful person's principles, choices and results in your field to aid you in achieving your own goals. It's not their appearance that we're emulating or their personality (except where it produced certain types of effective behaviour) so there's great potential for adding your own unique ingredients to ensure success is on your terms.

The best subject for modelling is one who's a model of excellence in the profession. (In fact, choosing a number of good examples is very healthy for avoiding singular slavish devotion). How do you identify excellence? Well, this is highly subjective (as heated pub discussions will tell you!) but it's simply a matter of who you alone consider worthy of respect and attention. Their level of talent will be a crucial factor, yet even more so is their approach to the work. Personally I find it pointless emulating an actor whose attitude is the slack shrug of 'Hey, I'm just lucky' or one who regularly sabotages themselves through drink and drug excess, (entertaining as those hell-raisers are).

Elegance, seemingly minimal effort and integrity seem to be common qualities amongst the most widely-renowned actors. Compare also their attitudes, choices and results with those of their contemporaries.

The next step is the joy of soaking up your role model's work, gaining insight into their approach and seeing their talent in full flow. If you're bold enough in your admiration, you could try to meet them maybe backstage after a show, at a book signing or even interview them.

NLP practitioners place great emphasis on direct 'live' contact with your model if possible. NLP modelling goes as far as replicating posture and breathing techniques to mirror your subject's attitudes. Their technique emphasises the importance of being around your model enough to allow selective behaviour of theirs to imprint itself on your subconscious. For those who find that a little akin to 'stalking', relax! I realise a direct meeting is not always practical (or appropriate) and sometimes takes a degree of brashness we don't all have.

Seeing a role model live in performance may be much easier and can still create powerful sense memories for inspiration. You can see their technique at close range, how they use their physicality and energy on stage, 'the unvarnished truth' of their talent. If you habitually study favourite actors on screen, take the opportunity to seek them out live. You won't regret it.

Failing that, DVD is proving a wonderful resource nowadays. Many discs contain excellent feature-length commentaries by actors of a depth and candour you wouldn't get in a standard interview. (Edward Norton and Brad Pitt along with director David Fincher on the *Fight Club* DVD for example are a lot of fun and very illuminating about their different approaches). Offering interviews, screen tests, documentaries about the nuts and bolts of the making of a film or TV series, DVD at its best is a digital education for the post Millennium performer.

Lastly but greatly treasured is a good old-fashioned biography or autobiography. Over the years there have been many that are now almost set texts for actors. I'll summarise the unique appeal to me of a handful:

Being an Actor by Simon Callow:

A very vivid, funny and painfully honest part-autobiography, part insight into the life of an actor. Recounts his highs and lows training at Drama Centre and there's a fascinating section that analyses the theatre process from first rehearsal to the close of the run.

Acting On Film by Sir Michael Caine:

A gold-mine of film techniques and tips from one of the most revered screen actors we've ever produced. Like a memorable afternoon chat with a wise uncle who's done it all yet has kept his feet on the ground. Recently updated and reprinted. Warning: lend it out and you may never get it back!

Beginnings by Kenneth Branagh:

His first volume of autobiography, published with admirable confidence at 29 (apparently to help finance his New Renaissance theatre company). Movingly recaptures his awkward upheaval as a child from Belfast to Reading. A very inspiring read for those looking to set up their own theatre company and for actors with the vision to make their first feature film (A rough diary of his filming of *Henry V* is at the back). Clearly beneath this affable exterior beats the heart of a man who was very determined and focused from an early age.

Year of the King by Sir Anthony Sher:

This is a year in the life of the multi-talented writer, actor and artist as he fused all his talents to create his famously dynamic 1985 portrayal of Richard III for the Royal Shakespeare Company. It's an immensely impressive diary, accompanied by his striking sketches detailing how the character developed. Sher's work is particularly effective, as is his later autobiography *Beside Myself* at detailing the process of how outside influences feed into character creation.

With Nails by Richard E. Grant:

An instant classic since it came out in 1996, this is the hilarious, bitter and bewildered 'Englishman-abroad' Hollywood diaries of the Swazi-born actor who shot to fame as the incomparable Withnail. This is the finest fish-out-of-water eyewitness account yet of the madness of making movies in the Hollywood ego factory.

True and False by David Mamet:

This celebrated playwright is the only non-actor of the list (although he did start out as one). Here he turns his attention to bursting many bubbles of perceived pretension about acting technique and 'the business'. Very controversial, as he slams formal training and dismisses imaginative analysis of anything, including the words on the page, beyond simple direct interpretation. On its release, it was a welcome source of hot debate and is actually written with great fondness and respect for our profession. As refreshing a shake-up of values as the Method was in it's time.

Everyday Boosts

As I said in the opening, there are always opportunities for refreshment and revitalising of our purpose even in a hectic life on the move. If you're someone who just manages to squeeze in all the demands made of you in the day, have faith that you can fit in the means of carrying out your purpose *if you want it enough.*

Aren't there times of the day where your body is engaged in a task but your mind is actually free to take in new things? If you do a lot of driving on your own, get a CD player going with some inspiration! Either music that fires up your invincibility or better yet CDs of lectures or courses on any subject that will feed you well. There are many great personal development speakers who supply live recordings and presentations of their books. Give yourself the benefit of new thoughts and empowerment. Over the span of a year, with all necessary concentration on the road, you could aurally learn an entire language in just the hours you've queued in traffic jams! What sounds better to you - road rage or an education? My car doubles as a mobile university, and disproves the idea that we men can't multi-task.

The same applies if you go to the gym. Running on a treadmill? Get some great words as well as music pumping through your brain. Add to that endorphine rush. Are there books you know will really help you but you never seem to have time to read with children around? Consider what time you get up. Can you go to bed an hour earlier, and get up an hour earlier? That extra undisturbed hour to take in great material is a lovely way to begin the day. (Since I started doing this, that extra hour each week-day has worked out at roughly fifty extra books read per year!). I'm sure you can think of other smart examples for enriching your valuable time. Whatever lifestyle you lead, the point is that if the pursuit of your goals beckons enough, you will find creative ways to support them…till one day they support you.

The Process

When our instrument as a whole is perfectly in tune, it's a wonderful way to live. We are pursuing a path in the present moment, going after what excites and fulfils us. We know at a deep level that this course is in harmony with the best in us. We gain huge pleasure from the actual process of the journey not just the destination. When one part of the journey is completed, we move on to the next, relishing the new people and experiences to come.

Our bodies also are responsive. We eat and drink what tastes great and serves us well, since we have no need to rely on artificial mood stimulants or suppressants. The big stimulant is generated within by being 'on purpose' in our waking hours, When we need to calm down, we sleep well at night without chemical aids because we filled the day productively in good conscience.

The effect on those around us

One concern people have about going after big ambitions is a fear that loved ones will start to resent them for it. We hear a strange persuasive voice that argues 'Don't ask for too much. They'll be jealous when you get it." Yet we know deep down that the ones who truly love us will not only be happy for our success, they'll be inspired to make their own big rewards just like we were helped by others.

Those who undermine you instead are revealing their true colours as people to be avoided. Do you tell everyone what your dreams and plans are? That might be a mistake if it means having to defend yourself against malicious put-downs. Who needs to waste energy on that?

I suggest reserving your innermost aspirations for friends and family who you know you can count on for support, and professionals who can help. Often actors ask for extraordinary dreams to be made reality, and if you're going down that road, you need extraordinary encouragement.

CHAPTER 5
THE CV

The most impressive calling card you have aside from your photograph (covered in the 'Agents' chapter) is your CV. Far from something to be timid about, this is an introduction to the three dimensional you. Your past acting work is the greater part of it but it's also a chance to show your potential beyond those facts - in your life skills. Actors are as prone to undersell ourselves on a CV as we are to over-embellish. We aren't usually shown how to do this effectively in training, so let's do it now.

The first key point to note in constructing an actor's CV is that it must fit onto *a single page*. Unlike some professions where you are encouraged to cover multiple sides with your training, skills and varied experience, here you must condense it all. You might well ask how to choose what to emphasise if you have more than one page of credits and in a number of disciplines. Later in the chapter I will give examples of CVs which 'cut your cloth to match different customers'.

Just the facts

Let's begin with the top section which is always the factual statistical data about you. It is vital to include the necessary details as an employer or casting director may need to zero in on this immediately when quickly making an initial shortlist.

Try this order:

Playing age

No need to put your real age as long as this covers the actual range you can realistically look (i.e. Mid-late 20s; early to late 30s) Age is not an exact science if the part fits, but be honest – a camera will.

Height

Hair

Eyes

Equity

Simply quote the number if you're a member.

Spotlight

See above.

Accent

Start by putting your 'native accent'. This is your own natural, unvarnished accent – Geordie, Liverpudlian, Mancunian etc. This is very useful information in today's climate that favours more regional flavour.

If your natural speaking voice has no regional accent, then put 'R.P' (Received Pronunciation) or 'standard accent'. All actors ideally should be able to do a standard accent such as the form spoken by BBC newsreaders. If you can't, then learn. Go to a voice teacher, imitate good sources – and don't claim the skill unless you have it! A put-on 'posh' voice in front of your friends is not the same as an authentic useful standard accent in the industry.

Then list the other dialects and international accents you can do *very well*. The same stringent rule applies here as to claiming the speaking of R.P. Employers have had their time wasted by so many "Tap a' the marnin" Irish leprechauns and "Och aye" shortbread-tin Scots that these days they demand 'authentic' regional types in casting breakdowns. Who can blame them?

If you were brought up around a native dialect separate to the one you have, make use of it. If you have a genuine ear for accents, consult those whose opinions are worth trusting and list the ones on your CV that are convincing. On that point, it's a good idea to make a mental note of any credible time lived amongst those of a different dialect or accent to give your claim real back-up. I spent three months surrounded by upper middle–class Jewish New Yorkers on a summer camp in New York State, so that helped me with an authentic facility with that sound. It also adds a little extra dimension to your history.

Singing

Mercifully, this is an area where few actors I know would dare swim out of their depth (In fact, they're almost proud of their inability). If you have the talent and training, note your vocal type and detail your bottom and top notes. Those with a singing teacher will be able to do this easily. If however you don't know a Tenor from a Baritone, ask someone who can gauge your voice accurately, put it down and don't claim specific notes for your range. That's for the 'heavyweights'. By all means if you're confident enough label your vocal style as a Rock/Pop or classical style. Again, you may only be required to carry a tune in a show, so assess your limitations and encourage the promotion of what you do have.

Roles in musical theatre productions should be listed under 'Theatre' credits. If you performed with a band, place it under the 'Special skills/Interests' section at the bottom of the CV even if they were a well-known group. Remember, this is a CV designed for the acting profession. The same categorisation and reason applies to professionally recordings.

(See the sample CVs at the end of the chapter)

Contact

Your agent's name, address, telephone and Email address. If you don't have representation and are with Spotlight, you can put 'C/O The Spotlight'. If you don't have Spotlight either (ahem - yet), then note your own home details including a mobile number.

Training

Your drama school and course are not the only qualification you can put here. You can quote relevant workshops and courses you've done and the leader who ran them. It might be a mutual talking point if an employer knows the person who ran that course. It also shows your commitment to ongoing training.

Mainstream early schooling such as a Home Economics GCSE wouldn't cut the mustard so to speak, but if you have a degree its worth mentioning it and including the subject as well. Some employers are strangely snobbish about formal education, and moreover if you're up for the part of a lawyer, a law degree puts you 'before the judge' that much more credibly.

'Professional credits'

Now that you've got the hard facts out of the way, let's deal with two general points about listing credits before we go into the layout.

Here is where a degree of flexibility works for you – that's *flexibility in choice of credits not description.*

Actors work in a variety of mediums and may need their CV to be fluid enough to exist in different versions to appeal to different types of employer. So rather than attempt to be overly concise and miss some relevant background, you will want to stress certain experience and de-emphasise others.

If you're applying for theatre work, it's a waste of space to list all your corporate videos or short films when you may have done creditable workshops or even relevant though small-scale theatre work. This would also be the time to put theatre credits at the top of your credits section. The exception where another medium feeding theatre should be highlighted is where you have had prominence in a high-profile television series or film. Theatre producing houses and regional tours are stacked with television names. This subscribes to the 'bums-on-seats' concept of tempting people away from the comfort of their TV set to go and see 'him or her off that TV show'.

If you're submitting for a screen part, then again use a version of your CV that emphasises your screen experience.

These general points will hopefully only really apply when your CV is light on respectable strong credits, early in your career. As you gain in experience and pedigree, a one-size-fits-all version highlighting the most recent of your theatre, TV and film work is a classy ideal way to present yourself.

Padding

Do not try to claim parts you have not played. Aside from never knowing if a name you drop here might actually be looking at your CV (!), directors and producers frequently know each other. I sometimes get asked in auditions, when a director spots a past colleague's name, how that person is doing these days and other banter which you do not want to attempt to fake.

Also, don't put walk-ons or stand-ins under TV credits. That section is for roles that you have been credited for *as a named part in the script where you received direction from the director.* As a rule, if you're not listed as a character in the credits at the end of the show, do not try to count it. To the industry trained eye, padding reveals itself very easily. If you lie and are found out, it casts doubts about the credibility of the rest of your CV and you could then end up padding somewhere else: *their bin.*

Avoid filling your CV with amateur roles. Save the creative spin for when you're asked about the significance of a small actual part you played when you're in an audition (See the section on Audition Kidology).

If you have only recently completed your training, by all means record the more prominent parts you played at drama school, indicating this under the heading *'Roles at X'*

Layout

The best way to lay out a credit is in one line, telling all the relevant facts as the eye scans across it. For instance:

ROLE	PRODUCTION	DIRECTOR	VENUE
Hanna	Living a Lie	Simon Pink	Leeds Festival

This should cover enough detail. If it's a television show, replace the venue with the name of the TV production company or channel if better known.

There are ways in which you can make the most of your experience without being deceptive in your credits. If for example you toured in a theatre show where only one of the venues was quite notable, you don't have to bury it in a nondescript 'National Tour' line. It's justifiable to single out the venue and then add 'National Tour' as in: 'Phoenix Theatre/National Tour'. After all, you played there! If any clarification is needed in the audition, explain then.

It might sound obvious but always make a note of your director's name to put on the CV. Theatre, film, TV and commercials all attract up-and-coming as well as established names which often cross over (commercial directors into feature films for instance) so promote them for all they're worth.

'Special skills / Interests'

This can be an overlooked area so give it a little attention. You may find the supplementary skills to your acting training are what get your CV to the top of the pile for certain jobs. (Consider those adverts that specify 'circus skills preferred' or 'puppetry experience essential'). Don't just list anything you're interested in - think relevance.

Do you drive? Simply note whether you have full, provisional or no qualifications and record if your license is clean. I would definitely suggest learning to drive as a skill; once in a while it can be a job deal-breaker. Friends of mine who can't drive find it very frustrating when they're right for a part in every other way but the employers need to have the ability shown for real on camera, or their touring theatre company needs an extra van driver. Learn if you can as soon as possible – it only gets more expensive with the passing of time.

Do you have instrument skills? If you were formally trained, put down the classical grade you last reached. If it was a long time ago that you last picked up that flute, be careful and realistic.

For those with dance training, quote the dance style and classical grade; it may well come in handy in a period piece. You might not have a recognised grade in any discipline but can pick up moves quickly, in which case list 'basic choreography'.

Are you fluent in other languages? You must only claim fluency if you can back it up on the spot, but by all means put 'conversational' or 'sight-reading' if you have the language to a convincing level for spoken dialogue. Short exchanges may often be all that's required (unless it's filming in that country) so if you had French or German for example *to a good standard* at school, then polish it and set it out in your armoury of linguistic weapons.

Stage combat is frequently taught at drama institutions. Those who trained in this skill will want to note the certificate level they reached. Don't worry if its not part of your skill set. A good company wanting to incorporate fight sequences into a piece will provide an expert with safe high-quality tuition.

When weighing up what else you can add, consider if it's a skill that can be used for a character, hasn't been mentioned already and is not something all actors can readily do.

Are there sports you play to a high level?

Can you juggle?

Puppetry as mentioned above is good to quote if you have it.

Even computer skills can be noted (PCs may be global but literacy with them is not!)

Overall, bear in mind since the CV and photo are your professional face to the world, to keep refreshing them continually. It's a good feeling to be able to constantly add new skills, training and credits, reflecting that you are always evolving.

There are many different layout styles for a CV. As long as the content can be seen clearly, how you choose to frame it is a matter of personal taste. There are many websites that give examples and even templates of varying presentations. What should not be left open to interpretation for the reader is the content. Make sure you disclose all the necessary details honestly in a way that the employer can digest at a glance.

To close this chapter I've included two sample CVs illustrating the less-experienced actor: the first emphasising theatre and the second stressing screen work with additional pop group background. In both cases they reflect an actor without an agent. (Once you have representation, they will customise your CV to suit their 'house style').

PETER HAYES

		Contact
Playing Age: Mid-late20s	**Eyes:** Blue	
Height: 6ft	**Equity:** 123456	48 Cornwell Close
Hair: Dark brown	**Spotlight:** 0054321	Manchester
Accent: Native Newcastle/Excellent R.P		M2 4XF
Singing: Tenor- A above Middle C		Tel: 0161 456 1234
		M: 07777 121212

Training

Three-Year Theatre Diploma – Monkbridge Drama School

Workshops with Damien Thorn (Physical Theatre, Actor's Church)

Theatre

ROLE	PRODUCTION	DIRECTOR	VENUE
Nathan	How Is She?	Maureen Wass	York Apollo
Hanna	Living a Lie	Simon Pink	Leeds Festival

Roles at Monkbridge

Henry V	Henry V	Barry Hester
Stanhope	Journey's End	Maureen Stoop
Porter	Macbeth	Howard Gordon

Special skills / Interests

Full clean driving license / Languages: Fluent Spanish, conversational French / stage combat (Intermediate) / strong swimmer /Rod puppetry

PETER HAYES

Playing Age: Mid-late20s	**Eyes:** Blue	**Contact**
Height: 6ft	**Equity:** 123456	48 Cornwell Close
Hair: Dark brown	**Spotlight:** 0054321	Manchester
Accent: Native Newcastle/Excellent R.P		M2 4XF
Singing: Tenor- A above Middle C		Tel: 0161 456 1234
		M: 07777 121212

Training

Three-Year Theatre Diploma – Monkbridge Drama School

'Screen Acting' workshops with Billy Gilbert (Actors' Centre)

Television

ROLE	PRODUCTION	DIRECTOR	COMPANY
Victim	Coward's Exit	David Beast	BBC

FILM (short)

Ben	G Means Ghost	James Varlos	Haha Pictures

Theatre

Hanna	Living a Lie	Simon Pink	Leeds Festival

Special skills / Interests

Former lead singer with *Chigley Mission*, (Top ten hit *'Love Fountain'*) Full clean driving license / Languages: Fluent Spanish, conversational French / stage combat (Intermediate) / Rod Puppetry

CHAPTER 6
AGENTS

Being interviewed by an agent can be as nerve-wracking for some as interviewing for a job; in fact more so since one can regard a good agent as a passport to many potential jobs.

Let's not get ahead of ourselves though. Why does an actor need an agent? This is a very controversial question as there are actors who feel they get along perfectly well without one. They generate their own work and handle their own negotiations. I believe an actor's need for an agent depends on the kind of work they do. I am in favour of every actor having representation, (I'll explain why), yet if the actor tends to work repeatedly with simple contracted theatre jobs or solely through established contacts with or without need of a contract, or solely in low-paid undemanding work, then they may not have need of an agency behind them.

For me though, an agent provides many invaluable services both to the novice and the experienced artist.

Bargaining power

Most actors, especially the greener ones, have no idea about how to negotiate a fee and acceptable conditions. Quite simply, they do not know what they are worth and may be too timid about asking for it. Someone new to the profession may be ecstatic at the thought of doing a TV advert for a multiple figure sum. "Wow!" they may exclaim, "*X amount* for a day's work!" Compared to many jobs this of course is easy money – however in the lucrative world of commercials, when this advert may be shown in a number of TV regions, quite possibly an employer may be getting away with exploiting the actor for unfairly low fee.

A good veteran agent will investigate the broadcast use of such a contract and negotiate accordingly on the actor's behalf. Their relationship with you is a key point as the agent can enjoy being as hard-nosed as they like in haggling with the client, claiming legitimately they are just representing the interests of their artist: "Its just business!" An actor negotiating on their own behalf is much more vulnerable and open to exploitation.

This 'good cop, bad cop' partnership dynamic used between actor and agent with an employer also works the reverse way. Imagine for example a producer forcefully urging a performer to sign a contract just before a show starts, or after a hard day's work. It's clearly not the best time to ensure you are going to study the content properly – and an unscrupulous employer knows this. This happened to me once after a tiring long day of shooting. I was asked to sign the contract as evening loomed and was not mentally at my sharpest by this point. I was observant enough to spot a couple of loopholes that were open to potential misuse and sent the contract back to be amended first.

From the hindsight of greater experience, what I could have done was to refuse to sign point-blank without my agent seeing and approving the content first. If the executives tried to make things difficult, this would be the time to say innocently: "If I sign anything without my agent seeing it, he will stop representing me." You've bounced a difficult situation back on them. Wouldn't want a reprisal like that, would they? This is a fair tactic to use since it is counteracting an attempt by an employer to emotionally blackmail *you*.

Also, to be fair to the employers, there may be times when complicated contract negotiations are needed with an employer of integrity. How many actors will have the knowledge to decipher contractual details or indeed to recognise and ask for what they know is missing? A sound hirer will welcome a wise representative seeking clarification of terms. There is more chance of an agent sharing the business language needed in dealing with the employer than the actor.

So there are three examples of the power of an agent as a 'shield' (or a knight) working on your behalf.

Fielding opportunities

Another vital function of an agent is in fielding job opportunities for the actor. A good agent often has a more sophisticated network of contacts than we do. They have the benefit of sometimes long-standing relationships with casting directors, producers or directors and valuable insider knowledge of these professionals' tastes. A novice or unconnected actor on their own cannot compete with this. The actor also may not have the time if they are tending a day job or are involved in an existing show.

The stigma of non-representation

Yes, it can also be true that some hiring professionals will only deal with actors who have representation. Either they've have been burned by frustrating experiences of actors handling their own affairs, or the actor doesn't satisfy this relevant scrutiny: "If she's so good, why doesn't she have an agent backing her?" A beginner has an understandable reason. A seasoned performer...? Admittedly, comparisons between agents (and their comparative location - London versus the North, m'Lud?) can be unfairly judgmental, but there's no getting around the fact that having representation implies that someone else in the profession believes in you - other than yourself. If the production company knows of your agent, how much easier will that be for getting you an all-important audition?

A stable contact point

This is a very basic common-sense note and it can make a difference. We live in an age of increasingly elaborate personal communication devices carried around with us, yet it's frustratingly not always easier to get hold of someone when you need them (If you know anyone whose mobile phone is always switched off, you'll know what I mean). An agent or their assistant will usually be a reliable contact during working hours just in case for whatever reason you are not.

Background

It's not just an agent's background in negotiation and opportunity-fielding that can come in handy. Some agents are former actors or come from other related backgrounds in the business. They might have first-hand experience of a situation you find yourself in. This can also be a great advantage in soothing the furrowed brow of the artist.

What type of agent?

"One that gets me work", I hear you cry. Well, there are two types of representation that you can have. Its worth looking at these options before you go prospecting.

PERSONAL MANAGEMENT

This is the traditional kind of agent as described above: an individual or team whose sole focus in their profession is the representation of actors (described above).

CO-OPERATIVE

This is a more recent development in the profession: an agency made up of a group of actors who run it themselves. At a collective level, they are their own agents.

This can be an advantage and a disadvantage. Some actors like the hands-on approach and welcome the chance to actively influence their own casting opportunities, gain more control of which jobs they are submitted for and to help others. They also enjoy the shared triumphs and commiserations of a little social community.

If this sounds attractive and you may have such a co-op in mind, you need to address some specific concerns as to how your particular one is run. After all, it is your work life in the hands of other fellow professionals. A name TV actor invited to lecture at my school about the business was asked his opinion of co-ops. His reply was brutal but had a point: "Look around you. Do you honestly want these people running your career?"

The only way to answer that is to ask around for feedback from current and ex-clients and if you can get an interview, do so – bearing in mind these issues:

What's the procedure for a submission? I know one co-op who will only put forward an artist based on sound judgement by two members.

What provision is in place to prevent abuse of the system otherwise? For example, members of a similar type sabotaging one another's chances in a submission?

How are other disciplinary matters dealt with?

How often do the members meet?

What's their track record of recently generated work? Who are they 'in' with as potential employers?

What do they require from each actor as a fair commitment of time in the shared running of the office? Is this run fairly? Is everyone pulling their weight?

Will new members be taught the necessary adequate office skills?

Does the co-op have an administrator or someone similar who can be a constant presence in the office? Employers can complain of always having to deal with a different person in a co-op environment.

To be fair, the need to ask around applies to any agent you may be considering. A personal management specialist can have faults, (favouritism to their famous 'name' clients over their less-well known ones, rumours of impropriety, laziness). Anything is possible, but thanks to the good old showbiz grapevine and the perceived 'six degrees of separation', you can always seek someone to help point you in the right direction.

Location

A dilemma for some actors is whether to choose a London or northern-based agent. This seems mainly to be of concern to actors from the North who also don't know if they should continue to live in the North or seek their fortune by being based in London. The best advice notes I can offer are these:

These days, the agent's location carries more influence than where the actor lives. As long as your agent is involved with the right people and can possibly network with them, you could live anywhere. I worked with a Liverpudlian actor who worked regularly in TV mainly in the North, had a London agent and lived in Plymouth!

Consider your 'type' and where you are best served. Are you a northerner or southerner? A northerner may well benefit from living in somewhere like Manchester and the more suitable parts and influence of a Manchester agent who can schmooze with the casting directors up there. You would also be a rarer commodity in the South though, which means less competition.

Reflect on what kind of work you want to do. For musical theatre, London's West End is the Mecca not only for shows but for regular open call auditions. For TV and commercials, northern-type actors can gain a steady stream of castings in the North with a good northern agent.

Think about where your colleagues and family are if you want to be strongly connected geographically to them. There's no point being miserable and lonely when you're out of work is there? Weigh this up against where you might get the most work.

Generally speaking, London-based agents seem to carry more influence in the industry, but an actor can make their name in another region through a good regional agent.

Leads

When looking for a first or new representation, start by using contacts of yours who already have an agent.

Are they taking on new clients?

If so, do they have someone of your type?

Can your friend give you an introduction to their agent?

Aim high to start. Why not? From your list, try to gain an in-road to the agent with the best reputation. You can always work down from there.

Make notes of which agency represents actors whose work you really admire. (The Spotlight directory lists actors' agents next to their photo) This is good for developing your business knowledge and for setting high standards for yourself for the future.

Also look at the Agents section of the annual Contacts book as well as search engines on the internet for lists.

How to approach

Whether a friend gets you a personal introduction or not, ultimately it's about the chemistry and profitability you and the agent generate together. So how do you ensure you create and receive the most credible impression?

When in doubt, see it from their point of view. A sole agent or co-operative of any credibility will want to see you in action before they commit to representing you. You would want the same. Make it as easy as possible for them to see you in the most positive and truthful light. Give them something to see you in! A CV gets you only so far. An interview is really a theoretical discussion to gauge personalities and intentions (we'll get to that later).

The introductory letter

Treat this as one professional writing to interest another in a working partnership. Often, inexperienced or desperate actors will convey just those very elements. "I'll even make the tea!" I read in one letter an ex-agent showed me. The cringe factor will get you nowhere. No-one admires neediness and sycophancy. Have some self-respect, damn it! The agent wants to represent clients who can be confident when a star-making part comes up with a big producer. If you defecate yourself now simply about meeting an agent, you can't expect them to invest in a high-profile future for you. Keep this in mind and you will reflect yourself much more positively.

Cut the waffle. Tell your story simply:

Introduce yourself and say where you're from.

(If you're a clear regional type, say so. If the agent doesn't have a Mancunian or East End Londoner on their books and can promote you, it will help interest them. It also provides a little detail colour along with the photo for them to imagine you off the page)

If you were referred by someone they represent, (in good standing with them) get their permission and mention them.

(Resist the temptation for too much flattery. The referral already says you're not just sending a blanket wave of mail shots to anyone)

Describe briefly what kind of work you want to do. If you have a clear idea of where you see yourself in the future, touch on it if you like. An actor with a vivid purpose is more rare and impressive than a thousand wandering minstrels.

Sum up how you feel this agent can help you. Again, resist obvious sheer flattery. This is a sober assessment of how the two of you could join forces successfully. Feed back to the agent any points you know about their working methods and success. Do it properly and honestly and its thoughtfulness will be complimentary enough to your intended reader.

Finish by referring to the contact details you remembered to supply at the top of the page.

That's all you need.

Over the page is a sample of how much can be conveyed in a short introductory letter. You'll find your own style of expression; just ensure it's respectful and to the point for these busy people.

48 Cornwell Close

Manchester

M2 4XF

Tel: 0161 456 1234

Mob: 07777 121212

Dear James,

My name is Peter Hayes, a young actor looking for new representation.

My friend Judy Norwood is currently with your agency. She speaks highly of you and recommended I introduce myself. I'm keen to develop more in television drama and Judy told me this is a very fruitful area of your work.

I'm twenty-six and originally from Newcastle. I can be every bit the native Geordie when required but I'm also very comfortable with a standard accent for greater range.

My base in Manchester is long-term so travelling to local auditions at short notice is very easy.

Please don't hesitate to contact me at my above numbers and address.

Thank you for your consideration,

Yours Faithfully,

Sending a show-reel

The show-reel is a slightly outmoded term in the digital age but it describes a DVD featuring clips of your screen work. This will sway some agents providing it's the right kind of material and is a credible professional reflection of you as a screen actor.

DON'T send a live video or DVD of a stage production (unless it was produced for professional retail sales in the shops). A 'homemade' video-recorded stage show usually cannot capture the live show's picture or sound adequately. It's for private pleasure – not professional consideration. An agent will soon become bored and slightly offended that they are being asked to judge talent from an amateur source. They will turn off the show along with their interest in you.

DO use clips of yourself from professionally-produced short films and any suitable clips of TV productions you have appeared in. These will usually be well-made and give an agent a much better idea of how your talent and range comes across on camera.

If you have these kinds of clips available, go for brevity and variety. Ensure the show-reel is no longer than five minutes in total, go for entertaining clips that highlight your range and talent and include credits on screen before each sequence. If in doubt, ask fellow actor friends what they would choose for you. They will hopefully use more commercial judgment than relatives and non-showbiz friends, (bless their well-meaning hearts).

The interview

Well done! You've obviously demonstrated enough chutzpah and given a good professional presentation of yourself to gain an interview with an agent.

What should you think about in preparation for meeting? As I said earlier, this is going to be a partnership. You do not work for your agent and they are not a servant to you. It is two professionals playing to their strengths to mutual advantage. This means you are interviewing the agent as much as they are interviewing you. They will also have this factor in mind. Have respect for your needs and theirs when you meet and it will set the tone for an excellent relationship.

A good agent will be looking at you commercially when you get together. Of course they know you're capable of great versatility, but to some extent they have to pigeonhole you. They must compare you to other actors they represent to ensure you don't clash in 'type'. They also have to see you through the eyes of the industry, as though they are a casting director, to understand how to get you seen for the right roles.

Are you a well-spoken upmarket type? Clean-cut? Could you pass for a down-to-earth blue collar pub regular? A young mum? If you've never been willing to consider yourself in such limited terms, swallow your pride and embrace it. Don't take it personally. Its just business and the more you are aware of how you are perceived, the more you can play up to it and capitalise on it. Don't forget some of our best-loved actors are those we treasure for inhabiting a very specific kind of role. When you come to power as a name player, or you are mounting your own productions, then you might call the shots and expand the perception the business has of you. Until then, this is how the game is played – on the employers' terms.

So let your prospective agent meet the real you. Dress comfortably and presentably in a way that reflects you. If you have a regional accent, don't disguise it to try to sway their impression of you. It could be a real plus point, and a wise agent will be a good judge of character anyway– your real character!

Remember in the letter we briefly referred to the kind of work you'd like to do? Here in the interview is a good chance to elaborate on that. Certainly an agent's first concern is to get you the most lucrative, highest-exposure work on offer (i.e. TV, commercials and film). That serves you both very nicely. They will care at the same time about what you really want professionally aside from that. It wastes everyone's time if they labour to get you seen for a middle-scale musical tour only for you to say "Well, that's not really what I want to do". They are not mind-readers, so help them!

If you have any stumbling blocks to being fully available for auditions its best to discuss them here. You may have a day job that's not the most flexible in the world, or, linked to the aims above, you may have your own theatre company with its own commitments. Let the agent know what they are in for as a relationship.

At the end of the interview, the agent may make you an offer of representation on the spot. They will usually suggest you go away, consider it and get back to them with your answer. Even if your instinct is an immediate 'yes' take the time to sleep on it. What's the rush? Think about the conversation and what your instincts tell you about how a working relationship with them might go. If you still feel the same the next day, then say so.

Important: when changing agents do not badmouth your existing agent to a prospective one. Aside from many of these people knowing each other, it reflects poorly on your discretion and maturity of character. Confine it to 'professional issues' and that should be enough. (The showbiz grapevine can poison as well as feed!)

Contracts

Some agents expect an actor to sign a contract which protects them from your leaving their agency until after a minimum time limit (often a year). A year is fair enough when you understand a good agent will make a substantial investment of time in a new client and it may take a while for their efforts to bear fruit. I would caution actors though about signing agreements that run into multiple years. This is a risk; if the agency runs into mismanagement or the relationship is soured, it's a long time to be shackled to someone unhappily. Having said that, if your partnership is mutually hopeless, you may not have a problem in being released!

Agency fees

What should I do if my agent wants to charge me a fee for joining? Simple answer: *you walk away and find a better agent*. There is no excuse or reason for an actor's agent charging anything other than the standard commission per negotiated job (typically 15-20% of the payment you earn for a job sourced through them). This is how they legitimately make their living. "Yes, but they have a website", the actor bleats, defending the agent's dubious case. No ifs, ands or buts - if an agent demands payment of a fee as a condition of you signing with them, then you don't join. No good agent would ask for an additional fee. It is beneath them and utterly unnecessary. This is strictly for shameless shysters who look to make their money exploiting naïve young actors. If you were on the books of a walk-on agency and were going into some form of publicity book, that may be a different matter but for feature-part speaking actor's work, under no circumstances pay a fee. Have I laboured this point enough? If more actors refuse to play along with this shameless exploitation, then fewer crooks will attempt it.

While I'm on the subject of sneaky costs, steer clear also of shady agents who trundle out this Trojan horse: 'We don't charge commission'. In my experience, this horse's mouth conceals a nasty surprise. Agents who claim not to take a commission usually circumvent the rules by charging one set fee to an employer for an actor's services and then pay the actor another set fee. Needless to say, these fees represent a much greedier cut of the action going into the agent's pocket than a fair commission. Have nothing to do with these dodgy deal-makers.

The financial relationship

Here, then, would be an ideal place to outline how an above-board financial set-up works between you and your agent. Basically, a reputable agent negotiates the top fee they can for your services with an employer. This is where you have the pleasure of backing off, secure in the knowledge that the job is yours, while they step in and enjoy the game of bargaining on your behalf. In work that enables a little room for negotiation, a confident and skilled agent can often settle on a figure that is high enough above a first offer made to actually cover the cost of the commission they will subsequently take for their efforts. (In other words, their efforts pay for themselves!)

The commission rate an agent takes from the actor varies between agencies and between types of job. Some agencies for instance will take a low commission from an actor (if any) on Equity minimum-paying theatre contracts and then a higher one for more lucrative screen jobs. Typically you can expect an agent to take 15-20% of the total agreed contract as their fee. The employer pays the agent the gross amount (minus National Insurance if deducted at source); the agent then carves off their commission and sends you the remainder. You make your own necessary deductions and then go wild in Monte Carlo on the rest (ahem).

Television, film and commercial work aren't just nice for the fees your agent negotiates at the time. They are also the gift that keeps on giving in the form of future cheques, (repeat fees, sales to cable and foreign network, DVD sales etc). Your agent gets flurries of mind-bogglingly tedious paperwork minutiae and payments (fourteen pence from a TV sale to Eire!) which they have to get some lucky book-keeper to calculate and pay you both from. Don't knock it though; cumulatively it's a nice little earner – and just in time for that equally unexpected gas bill that was in the same post.

As you can see, a good industrious agent with plenty of pro-active clients can make a living *with no need of shady up-front fees*.

The working relationship

It surprises me how many actors who have agents neglect the relationship, especially when nothing is coming in for them. Opinion may be divided but I believe there's a strong link between never bothering to make regular contact with your agent and never seeming to get any auditions! "If they have an audition, they'll ring me" seems to be the general attitude. Of course a good agent spends their working hours fielding opportunities with their artists at the forefront of their minds. This is not about hounding them or operating from a lack of trust; it's about keeping a good connection and getting a sense of what's out there and what I'm being submitted for.

If you're with a very large agency, I would say regular phone calls are vital if you want to avoid being forgotten! What do I mean by regular? Calling once a week and no more is sufficient. No agent wants to be pestered, and their time is valuable. To make the most of your call, do it in the middle of the week if you can. (There's no sense asking "How are we doing?" on a frantic Monday morning or discussing being pro-active on a Friday afternoon).

If you just want to find out the result of an audition, I would suggest leaving it and calling another time. Often employers won't give individual agents a result or indeed feedback unless their client is successful, (especially if they saw a large number of actors as in the case of commercials). Calling your agent after every audition is a waste of your time and theirs. Now that's a good time to practice letting them come to you!

Friends who do business?

So we've covered mainly what your relationship with your agent is about. I would also caution you as to what it should not be about. Although your agent certainly can become a friend, and a valued understanding friend forged in the cut and thrust of business, I would be wary of growing so close that your business judgement becomes clouded. "How would I know if that's happened?" you may ask. Let's say that since you began your partnership you've come to feel gradually that it is not working out for you. Maybe their ability or focus seems lacking, through a change in management style, personal circumstances, disillusionment or maybe you received an offer from someone with greater power. (Obviously the last reason needs careful thought because your current agent may have the past experience of 'name actors' to handle you to a greater level). Whatever the reason, if you know deep down that you can no longer rely on this person to represent you effectively, you have to think in terms of business. If what's stopping you leaving is anxiety over your friendship being broken, your agent's *personal rather than professional* disapproval of your actions, then you have crossed the line spoken of in the old adage 'Friends should never do business'. Remember this is fundamentally a business relationship.

One pattern of behaviour that might help is to resist the temptation to whine and use your agent as an agony aunt as some are inclined to do. (Let your friends and family have that) They are compassionate enough to know when you're upset about a lost job or the scarcity of auditions. It's not their place to hear your woes – or those from all their other clients who do the same. Let them do their best while you go off and recommit to doing yours.

Lastly, I would be wary of any agent who always prefers to have their assistant receive your calls instead of them. A lot of actors complain of this, mumbling: "Well, I guess they must be really busy on my behalf". That should be true in general anyway, but remoteness doesn't encourage continual confidence. Courtesy and the personal touch, when time allows, does. You may not need them to be a bosom buddy, but if not a friend, then at least *friendy*.

Spotlight

The most famous showbiz talent directory in the UK is still *The Spotlight*. Since 1927 it has comprehensively listed the industry's actors, actresses, child artists, presenters, stunt performers and dancers. Until the advent of the Internet, it was an unwieldy tool; a series of heavyweight hard-copy books whose details were frozen in time on the date of publication and had to be physically leafed through in a very laborious way. Nowadays it exists also as a much more flexible and updatable website.

Without wishing to sound like an advert, it is true that many employers' first port of call when searching for a performer is to access the Spotlight website for actors' details, inputting measurements and specifics and getting results very quickly. Rather than your agent sending out costly 8" x 10" photos with a CV when you are submitted for a job, they can now add an actor member's 'Spot-link' email link that instantly allows the employer to access an easily changeable on-line CV on the site. This could make all the difference in gaining you an audition slot if your job submission has been last-minute.

Membership of Spotlight is entirely your choice, but without it your agent's job of marketing you becomes much harder and slower. In a sense, Spotlight has become a business language without which many employers and employees in showbiz would regard themselves as isolated in today's high-speed communication network. It isn't cheap, but postpone a few nights of drunken debauchery (that actors always do seem to have money for) and invest in this service. You'll be glad you did, and in the words of frantic super-agent *Jerry Maguire* it will "Help me help you…"

Photographs

A good quality true-to-life photograph of an actor is invaluable to you and your agent. An uncharacteristic, poor quality or cosmetically-enhanced one is self-sabotage. All of us at some point have probably used the wrong type of shot. You need an 8" x 10" photo that lights you and presents you well. At the same time always ask of yourself: "Do I really look like this image first thing in the morning?" This is a good bench mark to judge from because you will often be seen in the flesh at the least flattering time of the day and never under the ideal lights that are painstakingly arranged in a poised studio shot. This might sound bloody obvious, but I've seen many photos that simply are not realistic and the actor then wonders why the decision maker seems disappointed when you come in.

Forgive me if this sounds sexist, but female actors need to be especially careful as they are more prone to this than the men. We're not talking about modelling here – save the '1940s Joan Crawford staring up at a soft light coquettishly' glamour shots for a movie role where that kind of impersonation is required. This is YOU. If the employer does a double take, let it be of delight because you're more beautiful or handsome in real life than because the photo promised ravishing beauty and they instead get a ravished 'wannabee'.

Choose a photographer wisely, one who gives you plenty of time and has experience of providing actors with excellent Spotlight shots. Ask friends, Spotlight or Equity for referrals. A good photographer can advise you on colours and designs in clothing that will reflect you well. (The texture of denim, for example, always looks good on camera) Certain shades of colour have particular effects coupled with varying skin tones and hair colours to create the most flattering and yet still very much true-to-life look that you need.

My own photographer is terrific at 'directing' actors through the lens in ways that convey their true character through their posture and the all-important expression in the eyes. He makes use of props even and suggests a scene's mood to act out. Bring your own music if the photographer is amenable to this. The whole point is to put you at ease and allow the true three-dimensional uniqueness of you to come out.

Try a range of atmospheres that convey you well but ensure that within some of those fun and even wacky shots you have plenty of good solid generic images to choose from. In other words, go for neutral photos neither happy nor sad, with your face in repose as if listening. These are the best idea for your Spotlight and CV images. Make sure there is life and warmth in your eyes and you'll be happy with the result.

Lastly, it's a bonus if the photo you have on Spotlight is a little different to the one on your CV for that extra layer of versatility.

Union representation

Since this chapter deals with representation, it's perhaps a fitting place to assess the value of union membership as another source of protection. British actors have just one union, Equity, which was formed in 1930 by performers from London's West End. It soon spread in influence and is now open to any professional entertainer. Joining Equity is not an enforced requirement; choosing not to join does not hamper you from working in the business. It is however a valuable back-up that you can call on for advice, legal expertise and a powerful sense of solidarity with fellow members.

Whereas your agent is there to provide personal bargaining power on your individual behalf, Equity meets and negotiates terms and conditions with employers on an industry-wide scale. Showbiz people have a tradition of being temporary nomadic workers, which has made us easy prey for exploitative management who could simply replace us on a whim whether we had cause to stand up for ourselves or not. As an official representative of such a vast proportion of show business, Equity has the clout to insist on satisfactory measures that contractually guarantee us protection against unscrupulous employers as well as impartially solving disputes between members.

Of course choosing to decline such union membership in Britain is your legal right, but if you perform for a company who don't operate Equity-approved contracts, you can be forced into conditions that only suit the employer - and not you. With no professional support system to bail you out afterwards, guess who's to blame for accepting the one-sided terms?

Like many actors, I regard Equity membership as a particular form of insurance; a silent reliable bodyguard whom you hope never to need yet whose very presence should warn potential villains to behave fairly around you. As with the other kinds of protection you pay for in life, you might begrudge the cost if it's rarely necessary, but it may save you a lot more when he steps out of the shadows with weapons you don't have to defend you in circumstances you didn't predict.

A memorable illustration from my own career is when I and a number of other actors once sued a former agent, (another link between the two subjects). It emerged that over time a great deal of our money was being withheld by him without us having the slightest idea that it was happening. It was largely repeat-fees and other sales spin-offs which actors cannot keep track of and accept their representative's figures on trust. Our union lawyer did an excellent job of recovering a much higher percentage of our debt than is often the case. Without their intervention we might have been lucky to see as little as ten percent.

However you decide to insure yourself against inequality, make sure you're well-informed. Some performers opt not to join the union because they seem confused as to its function.

A supporting artist I once worked with let his subscription lapse, arguing "What have they ever done for me?" I pointed out that Equity's website does offer a 'Job Information Service' now; I believe though that you actually have to make an effort to go and find work on your own. This leads us to the next part of your alliance with your agent.

Being pro-active

Whilst a lot of the time, it's a case of your agent alerting you to an audition they have sourced on your behalf, there may be times where you've found out about a job yourself.

Firstly, this is another great chance for the partnership to come into play. If you've heard of a show coming up containing parts that may be ideal for you, once in a while it could be something of which your agent wasn't aware. Here you can pass the baton and let them use their persuasive powers to hopefully open that door and get you through it.

Secondly, even if it's a job you entirely sourced and succeeded in getting yourself, your agent's expertise in negotiating a fee and conditions can be very important. There are cases of actors who find little activity from their agents and then resent paying them commission for a job they found themselves. What they need to bear in mind is the amount of unseen work by the agent that goes into submissions the actor never hears of, so it all evens out.

When good agents turn bad

Sounds like a ratings-grabber, doesn't it? Well for those who ever have cause to feel uncertainty about your agent's dealings, in particular financial disclosures to you, make a note of repeats, appearances on other networks or sales of boxed sets of shows you've been in recently. After a suitably realistic delay, inquire tactfully to your agent that you are aware of these outlets that 'we' should be reimbursed for. If they seem to have no knowledge of any payments, you can phone the production company and inquire with their accounts department as to outgoings paid to your agency. If delays cannot be fairly accounted for and cheques were cashed by the agency, then they are now in trouble with you.

If you find the agent stonewalling you, denying your claims and threats of reprisals fall on deaf ears, then approaching Equity for advice, including the harsh recourse of a law suit, (as recounted above) is the best last tactic.

With all these sober points in mind, I wish you a great and fruitful relationship. At its best, the actor and their agent can be like a great striking partnership in a football team – one crosses the ball, the other heads it into the back of the net. Teamwork like that can take you all the way to the top…so choose your partner wisely.

CHAPTER 7
GENERATING
WORK

Before we get into the preparation and performance of a great audition, a key stumbling block for actors is how to source opportunities on your own. This is especially vital for those who lack the resources of an agent.

Casting breakdown services

Alas, these are not job tow-trucks that come by and transport your broken-down career to the nearest employment garage. However, a good casting breakdown service will allow you to see details of parts in theatre, film and television that you might otherwise not have known about.

Whereas some facilities are only available to casting directors and agents, there are a number of pay-for-subscription ones that serve actors and casting professionals side by side. In Britain for example there are postal facilities such as *PCR (Production and Casting Report)*, Equity's 'Job Information Service' section, (see the previous chapter) and Internet-based websites like *Castcall* and *CCP (Casting Call Pro)*. Some provide on-screen casting details and also function as a database of actors' CVs for casting directors (and even agents) to obtain and contact. A list of email addresses is at the end of this chapter.

Save valuable time and money by exercising caution in choosing your service. In the past, there have been accusations against companies guilty of erroneous, purely speculative or even downright fictional casting information. Innocent actors have even borne the brunt of employer anger when they responded to site-leaked details of castings the employer wanted to be kept private. Since most actors make use of at least one network of this type, ask around for referrals. Find a source you can trust and you'll certainly enhance your knowledge and feel better connected to what's going on.

For actors with agents, ones who may even use some of the same breakdowns, it's still worthwhile having a reputable company subscription of your own. Despite calling your agent and finding they've already put you forward for the job you've noticed, there could well come a time where you bring their attention to an ideal casting for you that they may not have considered suitable. We're all fallible. It may have slipped your agent's mind that you have strong circus skills, or you may feel that a particular part is more within your range than they initially thought. Even when it goes no further than talking, discussing promotion with your representative using good quality sources increases your relationship with them.

Mail-shots

Sending CVs and photos to targeted casting directors is still a common method of touting for work. Many casters suggest that actors approach them initially in that way. It is something of a numbers game, and many of your submissions will go straight into the filing cabinet or bin, yet you can make your efforts more effective with the following tips.

When I say 'targeted', I mean be selective if you're going to post hard copies of your CV and photo with a hand-written letter. It all takes time - and money in the case of those photos.

The other approach is to email your details. Many casting directors' email addresses are common knowledge and can be found in the annual *Contacts* book published by 'The Spotlight' service. I would caution you on a number of points when using this very convenient method.

Firstly, construct a CV with a photo image embedded into it as a picture within the layout rather than as a separately-sent file. This way, you won't trigger your recipient's 'antispam' software, designed to flush out the 'other' pesky unsolicited attachments.

Next, to ensure the CV itself will not be treated as 'spam' and deleted, copy and paste this file into a blank email, writing an accompanying brief note at the top. The idea is that your intended party will open an email headed by an introductory message, scrolling down to a CV underneath containing a photo within that. Everything they need to know about you is under one roof and hopefully arrived intact.

All you then need to do to save laborious duplication time is to personalize each submission. Since my days working in marketing mail-shots, I've always found people in any form of business contact like to be treated with respect. Don't just change the receiver's name in the message 'Dear' line but also give them an individually-named subject heading to greet them when the mail arrives in their Inbox. A little relevant information is no bad thing either. Which of these would you be more likely to look at if you were them?

'My updated CV for your consideration'

Or:

'My updated CV Alex, for those authoritative white-collar parts'

It only takes a few moments to appreciate someone as a human being, and may make all the difference in them regarding your application in the same way.

Lastly, don't expect a personal reply due to the sheer volume of email your subject receives. Usually the only response you will get is an automated reply if they is out of the office that day.

Word of mouth

A very under-rated aspect of the actor's life is the sense of connection to others in the business. Not only is it vital for sharing that unique understanding of our crazy passion and circumstances, but it keeps us plugged in to the network of who's casting what, where and when. We can easily feel disconnected from the grapevine through our day jobs, illness or moving away from the perceived centre of it all. It's not always easy maintaining relationships with friends you worked and trained with due to time and the nomadic nature of our work.

Parties, showings, opening nights and other industry functions are potentially good sources of business contacts as well as amusing vol-au-vents and booze. Exploiting these opportunities and the right people to allow you inside is another matter - make that your business too. I sympathise with those performers who are not pushy and extrovert by nature – in fact, as I say in the earlier chapter on showcases for attracting agents, be sensitive as to how and when to talk shop. Ally yourself with friends who can identify or even introduce you to influential people at these gatherings. A little background preparation also helps, such as going on-line to view photos and biographies of potential contacts in advance. You can then pick them out in the crowd on sight, "Oh look, isn't that Ben Winchester?"

Another less daunting way to aid your contact-building is to look for examples of actors' websites that have an additional 'Forum' facility. Forums are a wonderful internet resource enabling members to interact with a vast online community all at once who have common interests. Using email you can trade information, hopefully dispel rather than be the victim of rumours and make new friends. This is especially welcome when you're about to undergo a long waiting period outside an open audition and would like some good company. That's our cue for the next section, so put out the word, meet your new buddies and form an orderly line.

Open auditions

The easiest and most direct way of getting seen is to attend an open audition. They fall into two categories: ones that are accessible to any member of the profession, and those available to the general public. Details of musical theatre open auditions, the most common kind, can usually be found in the weekly showbiz newspaper *The Stage*. As for the rarer film and television 'search for a star' style public castings, these are usually advertised in local TV, radio and press news.

Employers hold 'open calls' for different reasons. It may be because their preferred specific searching hasn't worked, or that the role requires the raw innocence that they would like to see untutored from a newcomer rather than an experienced possibly overexposed talent who can fake that. The 'It could be me' optimism of the starlet plucked from the crowd feeds the hopes and dreams of many, and a canny producer is well aware of the added incentive of extra publicity. The blueprint for this was Darryl Zanuck's famously epic hunt for the actress who would play Scarlett O' Hara in the film of *Gone with the Wind.* The studio's expert handling of this search began a huge groundswell of free advertising for the movie before they even started shooting.

Another factor is the public honouring by an employer of union guidelines: these demand a fair and expected viewing of all members who show interest in the parts on offer. This is most notably seen in America where an open rather than private audition is the traditional way of casting plays and musicals – 'the American Dream' in action.

Before we get too seduced, the downsides to attending open castings should be noted. The ease of entry can be misleading for a start. Weigh up the odds of success and not just due to the obvious volume of other auditionees. Since the potential for overnight discovery captured your attention, it may also tempt an unscrupulous hiring power to weave a deceitful version of this same spell of hope on other actors and the public after the cast were already chosen behind closed doors. I'm not saying such 'rigging' is common, but it is practiced on occasion. Put your personal agenda into perspective: production budgets now are so colossally expensive that a big theatre musical can cost as much to stage as a Hollywood film, so employers are under pressure to promote much more than just your individual career. Let your desire for that role burn white-hot nonetheless and if you are rejected pour on the cooling waters of "It's just business". There will always be other productions.

Equally, for the performer and the judge there is the patience required in the face of the sheer number of totally unsuitable applicants. The recent rise in televised open talent shows highlights this very clearly. For the sincere and dedicated actor, an open audition is a very clear test of commitment and, lest we forget, humility. Enduring hours of freezing-cold queuing outside a building with no idea of when you will be seen or the format the audition will take is a great leveller. Be prepared to tolerate plenty of ill-informed speculation by fellow hopefuls amidst the pleasant banter. You could well decide the resulting job really isn't worth tolerating this degrading war of attrition and head for the comforts of home, ready to fight another day.

I'm painting a deliberately stark picture so far by way of warning, yet for those who are prepared there are distinct benefits. Channelled through a mass cattle call against overwhelming odds as you are, talent is noted and may lead you to a private scheduled audition you otherwise couldn't have secured alone. In cases where the show's director is present, there's also the possibility of being spotted for an altogether different part on the day. It's all about using every avenue to make your presence felt. If your other methods aren't getting you in front of the key decision-makers, then you have nothing to lose by joining the herd here.

For novices, open calls increase your experience in large-scale performance technique; singers reading this might be accustomed to lessons in fairly confined rooms. In trying out for prominent long-running musicals, often you're presenting yourself on the very same stage that the show occupies, so take the chance to develop a physical memory of the cavernous space and energy it takes to dominate it. I vividly recall going to open castings for musicals like *Les Miserables* and *Phantom of the Opera* and feeling initially dwarfed by the gigantic auditorium's demands.

Gate-crashing auditions

So far we've looked at gaining a meeting officially through conventional channels. Some resourceful actors think they can bypass legitimate means by 'gate-crashing' - attempting to be seen by a caster uninvited. Any rare success stories using this technique have sadly deluded many a hungry actor. They read about another's ingenuity and simply believe they too can somehow break into a casting unannounced, blow the judges away with their talent and be chosen rather than thrown out. It's a lovely fairy-tale and up to a point illustrates the stop-at-nothing philosophy I want you to take from this book. However, this kind of guerrilla mission is usually undertaken by those who are the least equipped to succeed from it.

I don't encourage gate-crashing for a number of reasons. There's a world of difference between sneaking into parties or the VIP section of a nightclub, and blagging your way into a casting for serious employment. Getting into an exclusive social gathering usually only requires a little artful verbal subterfuge at the front door. You rarely have to prove yourself once inside, and if rumbled there are rarely any repercussions. It's a bit of harmless fun for an evening's entertainment.

For an actor 'going to work', there is the similar initial breach of officialdom and then what it takes *afterwards*. Every actor knows the 'chancer' type: the individual who falsely claims relationships or skills to gain opportunities. Unfortunately an expert combination of the unannounced glib salesman and the performer who then delivers on that sales pitch is all too rare. This is ironic considering that by our very nature actors are imagined as being gifted liars under any circumstance. More common is the tiresome 'wannabee' who pretends to know the right person but tragically can't pretend to be the right person when given the chance. They are usually ill-prepared, ill-mannered and waste everyone's time. Presumably, this is why theatre websites offer such stern rebukes as this quote from a regional venue: *'Some people try and 'gatecrash' auditions. Please don't'.*

The other crucial error of judgement is when an actor also disregards the negative impact their incompetent forgery has on others. They forget that desperate actions they carry out alone can easily backfire and ruin another's credibility. A reckless unrepresented auditionee only has their own reputation to sully. If you have an agent, an embarrassing unauthorised audition attempt by you will have the producers reaching for the telephone to criticise your poor unsuspecting representative and not you. Don't be selfish; treat the people who look out for you with respect or they may not trust a relationship with you. A wise agent will sympathise with your frustration and suggest employment tactics that reflect better on both of you. Avoid immature stunts and listen to reasonable alternatives.

Using your charm and confidence to influence professional access does have its place. If you have the gift of the gab and a flair for self-publicity, use it in either your telephone and mail contacts or social networking, providing the person is encouraging shop talk. This way you can ensure you'll be welcome when you show up at a casting and may even have a little advance bonding.

Showcasing yourself

Mounting your own work, if you have the resolve and resources, has a lot of positive attributes. It gives you a part in a show, which is always a boost for creative self-esteem and the CV, and also guarantees the highest form of control over the type of role in which you want to be viewed. Part of your self-promotion is in enabling casting people to get a 'characteristic' glimpse of your marketable type.

As far as choosing the type of show, unless you have a preferred medium be open to the fact that the stage and screen are shop windows for each other. Apart from the obvious economics of putting recognised TV faces into theatrical shows, live venues also serve as a highly effective talent showcase for the small screen and film (as long as the production is played in a major city I should add). For example, Alan Rickman's break-through film role in *Die Hard* came specifically from the director seeing him in *Les Liaisons Dangereuses* on Broadway. For his anarchic movie *M*A*S*H*, Robert Altman cleverly recruited almost all the main cast by simply transplanting the crack team of Chicago's 'Second City' theatre improvisation group (which later also spawned the young John Belushi).

Onstage

The most effective live platform for seducing your audience is an ensemble show. Allowing the cast to act with each other in a self-contained play or musical offers welcome interactive energy between its members and with the audience, and the useful realism of showing how good the actors are at working with each other.

A collection of individual monologues is received much less favourably by casting directors. Why? Think how mentally taxing it is to sit and listen respectfully to a friend's problems - and then imagine a long line of them *over a whole evening*. Is there any danger of light entertainment along the way, or for that matter any respite? One intense life story after another, even if some of it's funny, is not only emotionally draining to watch, it also disguises weaknesses some performers have in relating to others. There are actors who can do the most marvellous solo plate-spinning, but ask them to pay attention to another person and it all ends in smashed crockery. There is no better and more supportive showcase of your true talent than playing as part of a team.

The next question is to ask what sort of full-scale show should you then do to increase your chances of success? Again, put yourself in the industry crowd's mindset. These are regular hard-working people who've just spent all day in an office. Give them something they'd like and you'll win them over. You've been smart enough to avoid hitting them with fifteen separate waves of shock troops. Don't then spoil it by unifying but then hammering the poor spectators with Marxism, rape or womb cancer for two hours. After all, the idea is for them to want to stay and watch you for the whole show isn't it? I'm not talking about dumbing down or compromising on the work you'd ultimately like to do, (the above issues are all relevant), but this is a good time to take a bullet for the mass audience's pleasure. ("Bums on seats, laddie"). A comedy or light-hearted musical will be greeted favourably, and consequently so will you.

If you can't put on a full-scale production, then, if you must, get together with like-minded actors and do a showcase of scenes. There are companies around now who make a profitable business out of staging them for other people. These can have the double benefit of generating work as well as representation by inviting casting directors to see you as well. However, if you're going to put yourself in the hands of a showcase company, find out the reputation and past turn-out of industry audiences for their shows. Some are woefully ineffective and if so, your money could have been better spent on Spotlight submission (which you should already have, I hasten to add!)

A second cautionary note is that if you're mounting a collection of scenes instead of a full play, *use scenes with other actors - not monologues.* Apart from the reasons already mentioned, you'll never be cast in a monologue. Perform multi-character scenes. It mirrors real life and what you would be given in an audition.

As for publicity, don't expect everyone you invite to turn up, *and give them at least two weeks notice.*

If they do come, be polite, friendly and welcoming – and ease off on the shop talk. Assuming you've made the wise move of choosing a central location and a venue with a bar, an agent or casting director will be made very uneasy by pushy actors asking their opinions about them. Let these good people make up their own minds and approach you when or indeed if they want to. Most will prefer to go away and ponder and do not appreciate being asked awkward direct business questions on the spot. Understand their position. You'll no doubt have provided them with CVs and contact details in the foyer or by post, (you didn't forget, did you?) so allow them to come to you. There's no harm in a written thank-you after the event, mind you.

On screen

Recent years have seen a very encouraging rise in new film-makers getting out there and shooting their own scripts.

Partly this is due to frustration at not having their work funded by major studios. The other impetus is the advent of high-tech video cameras that now enable a filmic look at a fraction of the cost of film. In addition, festivals showcasing solely shot-on-video movies are gaining credibility, so if you have a burning desire to go and learn 'on the job' with or without a film-school background, the barriers may be less than you think.

Even for the budding hyphenate actor-writer-directors who insist on using film only, the guerrilla steps taken by pro-active pioneers like Robert Rodriguez afford much inspiration. In his enthralling book *Rebel without a Crew*, Rodriguez (although not an actor) financed his first film *El Mariachi* for just $7000 with only one camera, no crew and edited it between two domestic video recorders. This undaunted approach earned him a raw but superb first film as a calling-card that led to major studio work and a career that continues working on his terms.

Making your own film is not for everyone; it takes leadership qualities, great reserves of fortitude and vision, but for those with 'the right stuff' the path is there to be taken. Kenneth Branagh transformed his career as an international classical actor with his astounding debut film of *Henry V* (see the recommended books in the 'Inspiration' chapter). His was a tremendous showcase for everyone involved and had the double-barrelled impact of impressing hugely as an 'actor for hire' and conferring the confidence of studios on him to develop his next film projects.

Financing for such ventures is notoriously difficult. There are various public funding bodies you can research with strict guidelines that must be satisfied. In the private arena, funding methods can be as disparate and creative as the scripts they are intended to bankroll. Branagh and his producer made use of independent venture capitalists drawn in by a very professional business plan they put together. For those without such conventional means, Rodriguez for instance slightly alarmingly funded his first work by subjecting himself to medical experiments. There is also the uniquely demanding stealth approach - lensing your film in installments in between day jobs and other unwelcome distractions. Sam Raimi, his lead actor (and co-producer) Bruce Campbell and their team took many months of gruelling episodic shooting to make his debut *The Evil Dead*. They endured piecemeal location shooting under tortuous conditions regularly broken up by having to shave off their wild-man beard growths, put on suits and sell shares in the eventual product to family friends, dentists, indeed anyone willing to buy in.

Another similarly effective pioneering strategy is to create a television or radio 'pilot' for yourself. A pilot is a one-off comedy or drama script that presents promising raw material for development as a full series. The name is apt since your proposed piece could either score a direct hit or drop a very expensive bomb on the wrong target. Fundamentally it must be appealing enough in characterisation and potential plot ideas to sustain itself in such a format. Committing to an entire series is an expensive risk for a company, so making a pilot is a cost-effective way of demonstrating ideas and testing audience reaction in advance.

If you have the talent and dedication to write for yourself and others you can of course just submit your script to the drama department of any television, radio or film company. This is their chief means of connecting with new writers. You may be brought in for a meeting or subsequent workshops to explain and present your ideas in person.

A bolder pro-active option is to actually make a pilot with your own people. This direct approach can have enormous persuasive power if you find producers simply don't 'get' your concept enough from the printed word and verbal sales pitch you give them. Of course this method is much tougher, but will it be any more heart-breaking than having this amazing piece go to waste unproduced? Just because everyone's stonewalling you, it doesn't necessarily mean your faith in your script is wrong-headed; sometimes you simply have to get out there and *show* people your idea. What's the worst that could happen? Your pilot becomes even less made than before?

Put your frustrated energy into forming a creative team of the friends you trust and go to work. If nothing else, think of it as an ideal opportunity to stress-test the soundness of your script and forge strong bonds with the guys who may end up being a part of the future success story. Call in favours, borrow a video camera, ask if you can use your local community radio station's facilities. For every naysayer, there is someone else who recognises a go-getting spirit and offers what help they can.

Finally, don't feel you have to apologise for not having the same technical resources as the employers you want to impress. You are showing them by way of example, not by the same finished product they would create. You are doing your best to present the most truthful and polished version of the story you want to tell. Trust in this.

Recommended material:

Books:

Rebel without a Crew – Robert Rodriguez
(Faber & Faber – 1996)
If Chins Could Kill - Bruce Campbell
(LA Weekly Books - 2002)
Contacts - The Spotlight

Web sites:

www.thestage.co.uk
www.spotlight.com

CHAPTER 8
AUDITIONS

Here are techniques for screen and stage auditions that will significantly boost your chances of getting the job. These come from practical successful experience of how they are really conducted in the industry. I've divided them into three sections each with their own unique demands: TV and Film; Commercial and Corporate, and Theatre.

Preparation

Always remember - the employer *wants* to choose you. They want to be blown away by your vivid, committed interpretation and irresistible confidence. I'll guide you through the process, avoiding classic mistakes, and freeing you to prepare and deliver the very best in you.

TV AND FILM

Character Clues

Do everything you can to find out details about the character. Even minimal background notes make opinions, and opinions create the choices by which your auditioner will be impressed. Very often, you will not see the script until you get to the audition, so what can you find out about this person beforehand?

What's their job?

Often a TV part may have relatively small impact on the plot. Rather than driving the story as a key character does, you may be playing simply an incidental professional role in a main character's problems (their G.P, a police officer interviewing them etc). Small in lines it may be, but it's still your responsibility and opportunity to convey the right point of view even if there's seemingly no room for real creativity.

Knowing the character's job is valuable; it gives hints for a little mental preparation you can provide for their possible character traits within a scene. If you're up for a doctor part in a soap, the chances are you're the bringer of bad tidings (as mine have been). So, consider the potential qualities that might be asked on the day as you get ready. It's a great way of focusing the mind and creativity for later. How convincing are you at showing calmness, authority, compassion? Can you recite technical terms in a sight reading in a believable manner? If you have poor sight reading skills generally, then practice.

How do they dress?

A character's job often gives clues as to how to look in an audition. How you dress and alter your appearance helps compound a convincing impression – but be careful. This needs delicate judgement as you must suggest without being too precise. The director wants you to convey *the qualities* vividly, without imposing too rigid a visual idea. Applying greased-down hair and glasses to portray a shy librarian is too specific and will look like the work of a comic impressionist! A director will have to work past your imposed look and hope you can be versatile enough to take alternative direction.

If, however, you're reading for a soldier and your hair has grown longer recently, get it cut short and neat. There, you're replacing a liability with something generally appropriate rather than imprinting a narrow idea.

In short, it is your acting that mostly suggests the detail. Ensure your appearance backs it up while still leaving room for a certain flexibility.

Start with either a general smart or casual style. You may not need to go any further into detail than that. If it's a white-collar professional part, wear a shirt and tie, adding a full matching suit if it's a businessman. For female actors, portraying a high-powered lawyer would be helped by a corporate stylish coordinated combination. If you're playing mums or dads at home, consider what you'd wear comfortably in front of the TV.

DONT:

Wear stripes or spots. You may be videotaped – stripes and spots don't photograph well.

DO:

Choose plain colours, paying attention to those that flatter your skin tone. It might sound prissy but I tend to go for brighter (but subtle) suitable shades. Black clothing is not always a good idea because when viewed on tape it does absorb light. Brighter colours have a better energy and vibrancy about them.

Also, if you have a good figure, don't be afraid to flatter it with suitable designs if it's in keeping with the part. This doesn't just apply to women! Conveying a sexy rugged workman? If you have the body for it, find a t-shirt and jeans that figure-hug what the character needs to 'sell'!

If you don't feel confident enough to judge, ask people with a good eye for clothing. Relatives and friends can be helpful in choosing what flatters you the most.

Remember, when you enter the audition the director will make a specific physical judgement on you even before you speak, so do yourself a favour and help them to think the right way.

Your character's role and relationships in the scenes

I'm not going into acting-class detail here about motivations etc. We'll assume the most typical scenario, that you don't have the script beforehand. What we want to ask the agent or company for is something relevant and emotionally active that you can think about in advance. "What do they want?" (e.g an angry parent complaining to the headmaster about the bullying of your daughter). This isn't precious difficult actor behaviour – it's a fair question. You'd like information to help with your mental presentation like any other professional before an interview. You may not get it, but ask.

This also alerts you beforehand to any particular emotions you may have difficulty in expressing, for example anger. It helps you warm up and focuses your mind for what to expect.

Audition timing

Let's move on now to the organizing of your time, both of the audition itself and your personal 'clock' in preparation for that day. Regarding allocated time-slots, there is sometimes room for a little negotiation with the employer. Don't forget this is being laid on for your convenience as well as theirs. Just because they are giving out the jobs you don't always have to simply accept what you're given. The time you will be seen usually makes no difference to them.

For those actors who swear by competitive strategy as the key to success, from my experience gaining parts had very little to do with what point in the day I was seen. The only strategic consideration I would make is where the timing protects your best performance for yourself. You might request an earlier slot if you feel you're are at your best in the mornings, or perhaps later on if you have to drive a long distance from outside the city and need to freshen up. I would suggest singers aim to avoid the earliest starts where possible for the sake of natural vocal warming-up as the day goes on. If the auditioners can't or won't be flexible, so be it. You lose nothing by inquiring.

Personal timing

Knowing the time of your audition, it's always best to work backward from that time to the evening before when making preparations.

Get any ironing, bag packing and laying out of clothes done the night before rather than on the morning itself. Also ensure you have clear directions for your route. For drivers, if you don't have a Satellite Navigation system, the AA Route Planner on the internet is very good for providing a detailed route just from a postcode. This all saves last minute scrabbling the next morning and puts your mind at rest that all is ready. There's nothing worse than being kept awake by unnecessary worry gremlins when you know a poor night's sleep may show on camera tomorrow.

For a very early call, set more than one alarm just in case or add the alarm feature from your mobile phone. Power failure on both a clock and a mobile is highly unlikely.

Sleep well.

The script

At last! After all the preparation, the most important element you're being judged on is often the last thing you receive. Plan to arrive at the venue at least a good half hour before your call time, get your script and find a quiet place to go to work.

Yes, there's often a waiting room and some friendly faces, but you're here to put your energy into doing a good job. Fellow actors can be very entertaining company - and also a distraction. Be polite. Be focused. Let others indulge in that 'comforting' gallows humour of "Another one of these, eh? I dunno". Sharing common ground is tempting, especially if you're nervous. Consider though what you will bring into the meeting. You are an upbeat vibrant actor, not a cynical plodder. That brightness can make all the difference in how you're remembered.

In your focused mind, the audition has already started.

You also need to take the script away so you can sound it out unashamedly without hearing or influencing other people 'rehearsing'. Go outside if you can.

Making sense:
Information, Interpretation & Imagination

Information

Although it may be tempting to start performing it immediately, give the script a careful first reading. It's very easy to become locked into a knee-jerk surface performance that misses simple but vital clues. This book is not about teaching you to act; equally this audition is not the time for in-depth text analysis – so making sense is your first duty.

Go through the dialogue exchanges carefully. Do you understand who you're speaking to, what you're asking for and responding to? If you have a complicated scene involving multiple characters, it's easy to gloss over your relationships with each other. You may not have time to be detailed but at the very least *be clear of your point of view* toward other characters.

If you have lines that are open to different interpretations, make a note to ask. Yours is a new role in the show, and a good director will be only too happy to clarify what may not be clear. They'll be more impressed by an actor who feels the need to check what this character wants and then quickly delivers a spot-on interpretation than one who is full-blooded but hurtles right off the edge of a cliff. We're still in the realms here of information more than interpretation though. Keep it simple. This is to help in your understanding before you play the part.

Interpretation

Let's home in on the potential bear-traps. Are there any lines that are a real mouthful? Apparent tongue-twisters or lines which are easy to understand but carry a lot of condensed information? This kind of dialogue to explain things to an audience who may need bringing up to speed is called exposition. Soap scripts in particular, bless them, are very prone to this kind of scripting, often at our expense! It's up to us to make a convincing tune out of some very fiendish and at times downright unrealistic lyrics! Try this gem for size. I had to deliver this casually in my first TV soap part as a languid upper-class toff, whilst being the very picture of nonchalance:

"It's not every day a cocaine-addicted peer of the realm flees the country leaving a servant girl dead in a car crash".

(With an information superhighway of cluttered content like that, it's no wonder he ran away).

There is no finer way to stand out from the other actors than to inhabit a line like that and make it sound utterly natural and characteristic. This is another reason why it's so beneficial to get some space preferably outside; you can get some air in the lines and experiment till you find a reading that sounds and feels real. You may bring a literal breath of fresh air in how you present the scene in that stuffy room later.

Take the dialogue to extremes so you can select what works. Play with phrasings and word emphases. The jogger and the old lady will soon forget that strange person who keeps reciting the same thing over and over again and talking to thin air. How else can you hear what sounds right? It will sound fitting to the director when it's correctly understood and expressed. That may take the trial and error of bold emotional expression, not just intellectual understanding in your head which is really all you'd give yourself in a self-conscious space surrounded by others.

I don't believe that word emphasis is an exact science. There are word stresses that are clearly unsuitable, but there is more than one way of saying a line that conveys the truth of feeling. To me it's like jazz music where the player can improvise boldly around a definite structural line. Often we actors settle for one 'reading' choice which is sensible but emotionally dull and predictable. Give yourself the freedom and time to make the part live. The director may hear the lines delivered in very similar ways all day, until you come in and show an original take on it. This is why you came early!

Also, don't ignore possible subtexts in what the characters are communicating to each other. Remember, screen dialogue is written very sparingly. It's usually simple to read and deceptively bland enough to be open to missed opportunities.

As screenwriting guru Robert McKee teaches, a quality scripted scene is not necessarily about what the lines say on face value. I'm not suggesting you attempt to bring in a sack full of over-detailed motivations such as 'I love you but I'm not sure I trust you so I'm going to pretend I do and hold something back'. You can't play all that baggage and will only come across as troubled or the victim of indigestion. If you feel you are saying: 'I love you but I don't trust you' then communicate that – it's enough.

The bottom line is that you're aiming to do justice to the script, to mine the most out of it, bring your own individual gifts to it and revel in your creativity. Focus on that and you'll be a very strong contender.

Imagination

A competent actor simply fulfils what is in the script. A special actor gives more than is written on the page and in the director's mind. This extra ingredient between the lines is what excites and impresses the viewer and the employer. There is a backlash in our art nowadays against the 'method', but a sensitive actor can energise a performance out of the humdrum by using events and influences outside the scene as written. Allow your imagination to work on the situation and relationship dynamics.

For example, let's say you're reading for a TV drama where the part is a police officer seeking a suspect. You track them down to a hospital where they are currently a patient. You approach an on-duty nurse and ask to see him. The nurse inquires as to the purpose. You take out your warrant card, describe the matter briefly and once she is satisfied, she leads you to him.

On paper, that can be a very matter-of-fact low key sequence. If you are told that's the emotional tone needed in the audition, then fulfil it. More often, there is no particular direction given. This is a perfect open opportunity to add character detail, pace and originality – to stamp this part vividly as yours and no-one else's.

Let's zero in on how important the suspect is. A good director will be happy to address this with you. Otherwise, make a decision that adds drama and energy. Imagine this suspect is your obsession and you've just come from being bawled out by your superior who wants results now! Let that urgency sweep you in and affect your exchange with the nurse. (This is drama isn't it?).

Don't worry about the risks of introducing personal vision into your interpretation. As long as you are adding to, rather than subtracting from the text, your ideas will be welcome. If the director prefers you try it a different way, you're mentally flexible enough to simply adapt it. This also demonstrates your ability to respond to their influence – so that gives even more kudos to you. The point is that you're making remarkable choices as an artist, not a factory line drone.

Now that you're revved up with involvement, that's the right impetus for the next step.

The meeting

So you have the script and gave it enough attention to bring a creative mind to it. You've dressed suitably for the role. By the time you walk into the meeting, the aim is that your inner and outer selves perfectly match when it's time to serve the character.

Of course you should also leave room for the real you in there as well. A director would like to connect with the actor also, since this is the fun, bright and interesting person behind the role. In a high-pressure environment on set, a good friendly chemistry with the actor is more welcome to them than a 'method' performer's humourless shield of characterisation.

Allow the mind to relax and clear just before going in. Your seething cauldron of talent is bubbling away, ready to be put on the front burner when needed.

Knock knock. Who's there?

When you're called into the meeting, usually by the casting director or their assistant, you can expect to meet various combinations of people. You may see just the casting director on their own with a video camera, or in addition the actual director and perhaps the series producer. Hopefully before the audition you will know the director's name – if so, keep a note. Sometimes nerves send names out of your head when you're not properly listening. You might meet this person again and you'll want to remind them if their memory fails and you gave a good account of yourself here.

We'll assume you have a mini panel of three (You might even have more in a commercial set-up). You may not be told what the third person's role is in the proceedings; just their name. *Assume they are as important as the others and act accordingly.* This means that when the questions are asked, no matter by whom, *give everyone a share of your attention when replying.* Don't make assumptions that it's only the director who has the hiring power. In a series role often the final say is in the hands of the producer. And while we're at it, wouldn't you like the casting director to bring you in again one day? Good manners - enough said.

They're going to interview me as well?

Unless the decision makers are pushed for time or are perhaps a little nervous themselves (they are human), they may enjoy finding out about you as well as seeing how talented you are. They'd like a little 'colour'. You're not in a hurry, so enjoy their interest in you.

What are they going to talk about and how long for? Well, that usually depends how interested they are in you, so have some conversational ammo in reserve. It's not necessarily going to be all shop talk on the menu. They may be intrigued by your experience as a dog-trainer on your CV (I take it that was genuine) or in what you do for work when not acting. I was asked this by a director, and it prompted five minutes with him just on that subject. He was fascinated by my day work in another profession and I still got the job.

A typical open-ended question that allows them something of your personality and nature might be:

"So what have you been in recently?"

This is intimidating for the inexperienced actor. You could have a lack of credits and a nagging feeling of inadequacy. Remember though, the panel is not trying to test you, expose you as a fraud or score points off you. They and your agent wouldn't waste their time if they thought you were a 'lightweight' would they? They're engaged enough by you to want to flesh out what your CV doesn't tell them. They're giving you a chance.

Maybe you only have one short film to your name so far, and its spectacular release was confined to a jiffy bag through your letterbox. Not too promising? That depends on what you gained from it. Consider these empowering ways of regarding it:

What did this teach you about screen acting?

What interested you in the character?

How did it develop your skills and confidence?

Suddenly that little credit becomes more than a lone indicator of any experience – it's seen as a catalyst and a turning point in your future. The passion and enthusiasm with which you answer that question suggests the growing talent of an actor to be taken seriously.

So who deserves to be picked by this panel the most? The one who behaves like a low-confidence impostor waiting to be 'found out'? Or the actor who suggests they are a secret weapon waiting to be discovered? No contest – and you haven't even read for them yet.

Whilst in this vein, it's worth touching on *Kidology:* the art of using deception for advantage, (a.k.a. lying). It's used a lot by actors in auditions. Kidology is a double-edged sword - if you're not careful, you will fall on it. How far is a little stretching or embroidering of the truth acceptable and when is it downright hazardous?

Parts you 'played'

Be *very careful* in how you present credits on your CV as you may be called to account for them. A little finessing of the truth is fine. If you played a small part in a TV movie and the director in your next audition asks you about its size, talk about its importance to the plot, (It was important to you, wasn't it?). Every role has a purpose. If you had just one scene with a star name, mention the experience.

Don't apologise for yourself. You're a valid artist in the business. An employer may base their judgement of you unfairly on the scale of the part you played before, instead of your actual ability here and now. In that case you owe it to yourself to defend your place at the table with a touch of embellishment. You're not lying; after all, you played the character. No-one has ever suffered reprisals for putting a minor spin like that on a past credit.

Where you will scupper your credibility disastrously is by claiming appearances in productions you simply weren't in; the more high-profile the lie, the greater the risk. You never know who is studying your credentials and run a risk to your reputation. A naïve young actor I knew of was very pleased with himself when he blagged a free lunch courtesy of a senior BBC comedy producer on the strength of his impressive CV. As they ate, the producer mentioned one particular hit sit-com on the actor's credits. "It's funny but I don't remember you," he said pointedly in between mouthfuls. He was the producer of that very show. The actor's composure cracked like an egg. He squeaked in panic, "My agent told me to do it!" Hopefully, he learned his lesson.

Claiming special skills

This is equally open to benefit and risk. If you claim great facility with an additional accent to your own, make damn sure you can back it up because they will ask you to prove it right there (as I said earlier in the CV chapter).

There are cases of brave actors who've gained a career-making part performing an entire audition in an assumed accent. If you're sure you can get away with it and have nothing to lose, it's up to you. Georgina Cates broke into her first starring role opposite Hugh Grant in the film *An*

Awfully Big Adventure by auditioning using another identity and an assumed Liverpudlian accent. Convince the decision-makers and they will likely feel you will do the same for the audience and admire your courage, so the risk may well be worth it. Otherwise, you may embarrass yourself, your agent and perhaps your confidence. Think seriously before attempting such a stunt.

Claiming other special skills is fraught with traps too. Some parts may require horse riding, or expert knowledge of fencing or scuba-diving. If your heart is set on such a part, and you have no such ability, my advice would be to weigh up two factors before accepting an audition *and discuss these with your agent:*

a) How vital is it that the actor must already have these skills? Would the producers be willing to find the right untutored actor and then teach them?

b) If you're going to pretend the necessary ability, could you have time before the production starts to learn what's required to an acceptable level?

Certain skills may be acquired in the short term if given a period of weeks or months. This is how George Lazenby admits he got away with claiming all manner of sporting skills he didn't have when interviewed for the role of James Bond!

It's almost a cliché in an actor's arsenal to pretend special skills of some sort – (we are actors, after all!) Just be cautious and balance what is needed and what can be legitimately covered. Certain skills cannot be passed off, and wasting the valuable time of others may get you unfavourably remembered.

On that point, it just goes to reinforce the value of paying attention in those extra skills classes you may be offered in drama training.

Giving your best performance

A screen audition is a curiously artificial beast. You're aiming to simulate an actual performance, often while they videotape you, whilst dealing with factors than can detract from the truthfulness.

Let's deal with a few pointers before you actually do the scene.

A sensitive director will make the effort to describe the piece, the characters and maybe the tone for you as a guideline. They may also ask if you have any questions. Even if they don't, this is your moment to query anything you're unsure of in the playing of the scene. Don't wait till afterwards or keep quiet. Are you unsure of the relationships? Do they want a standard accent or a particular regional one if it's not made obvious? You won't be viewed as a troublemaker if you're checking something relevant that helps make a better reading.

Don't be afraid to ask if you want to deliver the reading standing rather than sitting if the scene requires it. This usually aids your energy and gives a much more accurate version of how you would play the scene.

Make sure you tell the person operating the camera if you intend to make any sudden moves (i.e. a quick entrance, pacing up and down while speaking, sitting down or standing quickly). They often won't be used to Scorsese-style revolves or whip-pans or anything more than basic rudimentary functions! Remember how important it is for this taped version to reflect you at your best.

For the acting of the piece, you'll very likely have to read from the script if it's too intricate to be memorised. Also, unlike a lot of theatre auditions, you will have to read opposite people who aren't actors. One of the panellists will feed you other characters' dialogue since you will be playing multi-character scenes, not a monologue.

How do you overcome these hurdles to create a realistic reading?

Treat it as a completely self-reliant performance.

In other words, as far as possible you generate it on your own. Firstly, when reading opposite a helpful panellist, it's not their job to be a great actor. They basically do the best they can to cue you. The wise approach is to imagine them giving you the emotional connection you need, almost as if they are not there. (You can gauge the reactions you need from your script work before coming in). Use the timing of their spoken lines but replace their feeling with how you'd want them to react with you. It's the antithesis of normal acting technique, yet it ensures you don't suffer from taking your performance too much from your under-(or over)-playing helper!

Also, let's say you can't completely memorise all the lines in the time given. Fair enough; we can ensure though that the tape playback still reflects us well. We don't want to show our face obscured by looking down at the script or giving shifty out-of-character glances at it. Learn any complete lines you can, especially the vital emotive ones. Then give the panel and the camera the full impact of your face and emotions when you punch home such crucial moments. This is critical if you bear in mind the ultimate decision-maker may not be in the room and has to rely solely on the tape for their decision.

So there you have the elements that make up the typical TV and film audition. There are other types of screen auditions that have their own peculiarities. That leads us to our next section.

COMMERCIALS AND CORPORATE

The main difference separating TV commercials and corporate DVDs from mainstream television and film is that you are there to promote a company and their products. If this blatant use of yourself for capitalistic purposes fills you with revulsion, well no-one's forcing you to do them. Maybe your agent is very insistent, driven by the lucrative commission, but if they're pushing you against your will then have a word with them about what it means to work *together*.

Let's assume the client themselves don't conflict with your principles. With that as a compass, here are some pointers on a great way of making a lot of money for a very small amount of work, having fun and working with some talented and potentially up-and-coming names in the business.

The client psychology

From this point, I'll just use the term 'advert' to describe both mediums except where I need to discriminate.

As I've just said, commercials and corporate work are a reflection of a company and their product. In a TV advert, you are selling them and their image to the general public as purveyors of high quality items and services the public should want and trust. In a corporate DVD, the image is the same but you are preaching to a more specific audience, namely targeted business clients or the actual employees within a company itself in the case of a training DVD. These are obviously not meant for the public to see. The bad news for us is this much smaller audience translates into a much smaller fee for us, but I guess those gold bath-taps can wait.

Ironically, to promote a firm's honesty and integrity to other businesses, itself or the public, they will usually hire actors to fake it for them! That's the good news for us. This is a lot cleverer and more ethical than it sounds. If you've ever seen an overweight shifty slob in an ill-fitting suit or an 'Honest John' wide-boy as the front man for a legal firm or used car dealership, it's no use sputtering "I wouldn't buy a roll of toilet paper from him! Where did they get this guy?" The chances are 'they' are 'him'. He is quite possibly the

Ian Champion

owner of the company and had convinced himself (and the hands-tied ad agency) that his sincerity and appearance in real life will translate effortlessly onto screen. Very brave, but also a catastrophic waste of a huge amount of money if he looks uncertain, forced or phoney. If you ask most civilians to play themselves on camera, they don't know how to do it! This is where we come in – to be them more effectively on screen than they could be.

With the help of a wise and experienced advertising agency, a package will be put together for the client. This comprises a good script summing up the company's message with brevity, humour and impact, a sensitive and imaginative director (please) and actors that match the characters needed.

I've noticed two styles of adverts that actors are offered. I'll call them 'The Story' and 'The Spokesperson'.

'The Story'

This is where a conventional dramatic or humorous story is told, such as the householder bemoaning their chewing-gum grey laundry before Brand X magically appears. These are shot in either a heightened, deliberately make-believe way or designed to reflect as much as possible the lifestyles of the audience.

They are cast in a traditional way that has a lot in common with typical TV since you are actually playing a character. They'll be looking for believable fictional

171

character parts and couples with convincing chemistry (more on that a little later), whilst at the same time making use of an actor's typical 'type'. With only thirty seconds to tell the whole plot, an easily identifiable character saves precious screen time. They can also be fun and good training for the actor when the script uses all-important humour and absurdities such as sight gags. A successful funny advert is like appearing in a good comedy sketch. You can be proud of it and it's a handy wide-release rotating showcase for casting directors to see you in.

'The Spokesperson'

This is a different discipline. Here, the actor is required to speak directly to the audience as the representative of the company. In a sense it's less artificial since you are seemingly 'yourself' as the speaker and are mainly focused on the delivery of straight 'factual' speech about the company's product or service.

Find specifics about the character

My notes on preparing background for a TV audition apply, but here even more is at stake in the first impression than in TV drama.

You must get the essence of what they're projecting *immediately*. The client's snap judgements will be even more precise than the audience's because you're reflecting them and their idealised image of their customers.

If you're unlucky enough to hear any of their notes, just pay attention to the ones where you failed to create the impression you thought you had. Concerning the rest? Ignore them. It's just business. One person's perception of 'rough' is another's welcome portrayal of 'down to earth':

"Are they good-looking enough to be one of us/one of our customers?"

(Not much I can do about that except make the most of myself and be likeable me! If they're being superficial, I don't want to work for them).

"We want the average bloke down the pub. That's our target audience".

(Good. My agent said to go casual. Everyone says I'm really matey so I'll just be myself).

"We want a stylish well-groomed type".

(Good thing I wore the designer suit. I saw from their website how smart they are. It makes me feel confident and professional -and a bit sexy).

"We're not into the corporate image. He looks too high-powered".

(Rats! I knew I should have dressed down a little. I look good in a suit but it's not what they asked for).

"The accent was a bit abrasive, wasn't it? Might be a bit downmarket for us"

(I thought I'd use my own accent. I should have asked what they wanted; I could have toned it down a little. I didn't know...*Sound of unfortunate pet being booted*)

"A good solid no-nonsense Yorkshireman. Plain speaking. None o' these posh London airs and graces. You can trust him. He's the one."

(I'd seen their ads before. They're very keyed into reflecting their community. The character's a mechanic, a working man not afraid to get his hands dirty. He'd sound like me. I got it spot on).

Partnering

If you're being partnered with someone to go in as a couple, give yourself a fighting chance by getting as much time as possible to connect and find some rapport with each other. Even if you've met before, one of you might be having a hard day, so ease each other's nerves and preoccupations. Let the casting people see a good real chemistry of two people working together. You're dependent on each other to succeed.

Technique tips for being a spokesperson

When you're playing a spokesperson, you may need more time to go over the script than normal. This is because you'll very likely be doing a monologue to camera promoting the firm.

Promote your qualities – the product will sell itself.

A monologue to camera is a direct approach: sincere undiluted impact from one human being to another.

Instead of playing the lines as another character, you're imbuing them with important 'qualities' from inside you. These are qualities every firm wants to have associated with their brand. They will come not from the product, but from you.

As every good salesman knows, they are not selling the product but themselves. These qualities are:

Sincerity

Authority

Warmth

Understanding

When the audience likes and trusts you, they trust the humanity of the company.

An advertiser's script should be a platform for an actor to demonstrate all these four qualities. If the advert doesn't feature them, *add them to your performance yourself* and watch how that wins over the client.

If you think this sounds too much of a 'one-size-fits-all' formula, imagine acting a speech with NO in front of any of the four qualities above – Wouldn't go down very well, would it?

The beauty of applying an interpretative model like this to advert monologues is that it allows you to fill in gaps of light and shade where sometimes the writing doesn't have enough. The words are a springboard for positive feelings and connections. You're able to give the speech more than it might pull out of most people. You may feel as you recite it the stirrings of Henry V at Agincourt. (Many companies strive for a triumphant world-dominating sense in their adverts). Feel those qualities course through you as you represent the firm.

Addressing the camera

Since you're speaking directly to the camera, here's a perfect opportunity to show how comfortable your relationship is with it.

Think of the lens as though it's a single person - a loved one or a friend.

Tell them about the service because you care about helping them. This avoids the overblown artificiality of addressing a wide audience. It conveys an easy friendship (and intimacy when appropriate) that makes every viewer feel they are being appealed to as an individual. Relating to the audience like this invests your voice and eyes with seductiveness and warmth, qualities that the camera always captures. It also puts your attention where it belongs, rather than on the potentially intimidating panel scrutinising you!

Practise this technique at home. Take speeches from TV adverts and deliver them to the cat or an inanimate object. Treat your listener as that special someone – and take your time.

Stamping the brand

Another vital element to focus on is *the spoken brand name* of the company. All firms want their product or name mentioned, and all with the most favourable associations. They want to be regarded as a confident, sexy, powerful market leader. Get their psychology into your performance. Look for the scripted opportunities where you mention their name and say it as though it represents something truly remarkable. In close-ups, the decision-makers respond to that. You're flattering their perception of themselves.

The lighter side: the embarrassment factor

One other peculiarity about commercial auditions is how often you'll be asked to enact the most bizarre scenarios. Advertisers will stop at nothing to be memorable and amusing. There'll be times where you feel like a clown in more ways than one. Suck up the 'degradation', think of the money and just go for it. You may enjoy it. My own rogue's gallery includes making love to a pushbike naked (don't ask), and playing a marathon runner attacked by a giant tuna fish. In one of my filmed adverts, I force-fed myself fake coffee granules from a huge tin and slapped myself silly to convey desperate alertness. They can be lucrative and a lot of fun.

Patience

Commercial makers see many more actors than the television or corporate people. They often work from a very broad idea of what they need, so by necessity you will be one of a long list of people to be seen. This needn't discourage you. Just bear in mind the decision may take longer - if indeed one comes back at all. In two of the adverts I scored with, it took a fortnight to find out I'd been cast. In both cases, I'd forgotten about them, focusing healthily on what was next instead of obsessing about a result I had no control over.

Networking

Since the 1960s, we've seen the rise of the hotshot screen director who began their career in glossy commercials then went on to make their own feature films and television. Many, such as Ridley Scott, Russell Mulcahy and Tony Kaye still return to do interesting and fun assignments.

Also, there are British directors like Shane Meadows who began in film and then came to commercials later. It's a very creatively fertile ground for them, offering big budgets, elaborate preparation and shooting for a very such short running time. This also makes them very worthwhile for actors' CVs and the possibility of future favourable contacts for bigger projects.

THEATRE AUDITIONS

So far I've covered a lot of key points that apply across the board to all auditions. You can refer back to the 'Training' section for thoughts on how to choose theatre audition speeches. However once out in the professional theatre, there are unique conditions to understand.

One noticeable change in recent years is that the requirement for general audition speeches is increasingly outdated. I auditioned for a director at a major provincial theatre some time ago and she was surprised it still happened. For her, like many directors now, there seems little point in asking for pieces that would be unrelated to the planned production, especially if the actor may have no idea what he is being considered for!

They already assume we can act. Some form of vetting was done before allowing us through the door. What a director wants to know is "Can I get on with this person for the necessary six weeks or six months? Could we see eye-to-eye and maybe have some fun?" Or will 'Break a leg' become a sincere wish?

Choosing speeches

There will be times when you're asked for separate speeches and you may have a very good idea of the play and part on offer. This end result needs a more canny thought process than your drama school speech choices.

Obviously you'll work hard on impressing them for the designated play. At the same time, look for other monologues suitable for that character but slightly less direct. The aim is to whet their appetite for what you would do under their play's circumstances. If you know what play is on offer yet don't know which actual character they are seeing you for, find a play with a part to match the other play's role. Is this going to be a searing political diatribe? Will it be a loose, energetic farce? Oscar Wilde? Choose accordingly.

When I joined a regional touring theatre company in 2003, it was via an audition where my advance knowledge was limited. I knew it was a new play about the harrowing Battle of Stalingrad, and that I would be one of three actors doubling as both Nazi and Russian soldiers as the focus switched from one camp's fortunes to the other. I wasn't privy to a script for it except one speech I was given to work on. This was a self-contained ghost story so even that tantalisingly told me little about the character speaking. I was also asked to prepare a chosen monologue of my own.

The director had impressed on me how grim and raw the play would be, so it was time to go through my repertoire of speeches. Hallelujah! One of my favourites was from John

Pielmeier's *The Boys of Winter*, set in the Vietnam War. It's a blistering verbal attack by a Private on his commanding officer following a tragic incident involving one of his men. My gut instinct told me its tone and content would be suitably in alignment. There is no right or wrong as to where you choose monologues from as long as the piece flows well, shows character and is dramatic. It's a good idea to keep abreast of new plays and playwrights out there for material, being aware that you may not be the only one considering it.

Be wary of composing monologues edited together from bitty snatches of dialogue in a scene with another character. Unless it forms a continuous through-line of thought, it'll be uneven and unsatisfying to your audience. They're also fiendish to perform since they have no overall structure to lock onto.

Ideal structure for speeches

A good benchmark is to look for a piece that can be lifted out of context and will still make sense to someone unfamiliar with the overall play. A great example is a story told by a character. It has a definite beginning, middle and end allowing you to build a shape and rhythm to a clear climax. You can also create great and memorable images that linger. Everyone likes a good story well told.

Presentation

Let your audience feel they are in the hands of a confident professional.

Prepare your audience with a touch of background if a monologue may be unfamiliar to them. Nothing elaborate, just say for instance: "This is Ray Wilson from *Midnight Men*. He's a school teacher who's just come home to find his wife in the arms of another man". Rehearse in advance a brief description you'll say if the need arises. Directors often ask and make a note if the play interests them.

Give yourself a moment to gather your focus before launching into the speech. Even if you can turn it on like a tap, a pause first is an effective separation between you and the performance.

Ensure you give a definite ending: a gesture, a freeze, a relaxing of a posture, something that signals the monologue is done. I've seen many a good speech harmed by a woolly ending that's slightly embarrassing for the actor and audience. Again, it lets the judge relax in the hands of a confident artist who communicates clearly.

The aftermath of any audition

So you've been in, met your prospective employer and, all being well, left them with a great impression. Let's give a little attention now to the impression the audition left on you.

I find generally that if I've done the best I could, it's very easy to let go of the experience. When I've sold myself short, the audition lingers by making me replay it repeatedly as if I were trying a second time. Don't over-analyse; just think how you might improve for the next one.

The chances are that your inability to let go of it is the mind wanting you to learn something. What happened during the monologue? Did you gabble your answers to questions? Did you talk too much and listen too little? Spend just enough time on a post-mortem to pick out what needs working on – we can all use a bit of fine tuning to our engines. Glaring errors can be addressed. No need to torture yourself over an elementary mistake; just don't do it again. Maybe there are technical issues: your sight-reading, short term memory etc. Now is the time to put into practice the art of learning to be better. It takes the mind off self-flagellating and immediately puts the attention to more positive purpose.

The other unhealthy fixation is to read too much into *praise*. As the saying goes, actors can die of encouragement. The audition panel might shower you with compliments about your work. These are lovely to hear - but keep your head in reality. I was once told after a commercial audition: "I don't think we'll see that done better today". Well, it looks like he was wrong because that part went to someone else. Until you are told the job is yours, just be grateful, be inspired, and them move on to what's next, just the same as if you heard nothing. You have no control over who else they are seeing after you, or how effusive they may be with everyone! It's not our place to second-guess their minds.

On that note, the same steady heart applies to the curious world of *'pencilling'*. A very common result of an audition, rather than a straight answer, is for you or your agent to be told you've been 'lightly' or 'heavily' pencilled in. These are simply degrees of hedging their bets. They like you, aren't sure, yet want you to know the level to which you're in with a good chance. More so even than an unknown result, this needs even greater reserves of shrugging and moving on than the usual wait. There is even the possibility you could be told you have the job, then be reverted back to pencilled status, and so on until someone in authority has the courage of their convictions. It's just business, and since you cannot influence the outcome, then get on with your life and let the chips fall where they may.

Casting breakdown resources:

Castnet - *www.castnet.co.uk*

Casting Call Pro - *uk.castcallpro.com*

Castcall – www.castcall.co.uk

Equity – www.equity.org.uk

PCR – *www.pcrnewsletter.com*

Shooting People – *www.shootingpeople.org*

CHAPTER 9
LEARNING LINES

O
ne of the most common questions members of the public ask us is "Have you been in EastEnders?" If I'm still listening afterwards, another is "How do you learn all those lines?" Here is a method for those who are a little anxious about memorising dialogue, especially when faced with the big roles. These are borne of my teenage years in my local Youth Theatre and my exam crises at school.

Linking words

In my early teens when I took myself seriously but not theatre, (an ill-advised combination), I used to learn lines in whole sentences by reciting them out loud or by repeating them in scenes whilst rehearsing. Both approaches were frustrating. The first method created set patterns of emphasis that resisted flexibility, and the second meant spending rehearsal scenes studying the text instead of my co-actors.

In my Youth Theatre, our director encouraged us in a very powerful and respectful method of line-learning:

*First, find a quiet place and be without any distracting influences, including drinks.

*Then take the text and one at a time sound the words out (without emotion), hearing each one individually and clearly. Then add the next until you come to a punctuation point or sentence end.

*At each natural break, then recite the group of words you have so far altogether, still resisting the urge to 'act' them with any emotion. This begins a chain of words that will gradually weave into a long unbreakable line of recall.

For instance, take this section from *Measure for Measure*:

'Be absolute for death: either death or life
Shall thereby be the sweeter. Reason thus with life:
If I do lose thee, I do lose a thing that none but fools
would keep'.

Here, you could begin with 'Be' then take each separate word to the colon of the first 'death', recap that little section and then go from 'either' to 'sweeter'. Summarise now the entire line and a half and move on to 'Reason'. It may seem slow, yet this methodical sureness will pay off. The carving up into small naturally breaking sections allows you to make intellectual sense of what you're learning for when you put the emotion through it 'on its feet' later.

(One note of caution, particularly with older texts - ensure punctuation points are in places you want them to be. Punctuation in Shakespeare for example was imposed by later editors, not by him. You may want to erase it from the page and put in your own choices. Just be sure it works for you in learning and performing)

This technique reinforces your memory of the information but also uses the spoken sound of the word to embed it further into your mind. The respectful part is that as you go along you'll pay attention to the writer's choice of certain words and expressions that might otherwise be glossed over in more glib learning methods.

The next step is structuring the sessions.

Linking sessions

When I was preparing for my A-level exams I needed to revise reams of facts and quotes and remember them under exam pressure. Since cheating is not an approved option I found a brilliant book by Tony Buzan called *Make the Most of Your Mind*. This little volume revolutionised my learning for life in its explanation of how the memory works. He noticed that we have our most vivid recall at the beginning and end of any session we spend memorising. No matter how long we try to hammer facts into the brain, (and the longer we spend at one sitting, the more ineffectively stressful it is), it's the start and finish that stays with us the most. The trick then is to break up your line learning sessions into as many chunks as possible to take advantage. Typically I would do *no more than twenty minutes at a time.*

The other point I found from experience is that the time you spend away from the learning is as valuable as the time you devote to it. A five minute break between each twenty minute burst allows space for the facts to settle and somehow enables the mind to invisibly strengthen the chain.

When you come back to begin a new learning block, quickly recite what you've learned up to this point - if it's not too large an amount. The confident recall of all that's gone before is a great motivator to keeping you going.

Coupling these two methods together for the words and the sessions enabled me to revise an entire two year A-level course, (prepared on cue cards over the previous two weeks), in eight hours on the actual day of an exam.

Give these techniques a go. They may aid you in vividly embedding lines into your mind in a linked way that allows you to pick up the 'chain' at any point and recall the rest.

To recap*:*

*Structure line-learning time into 20 minute blocks, with a 5 minute break in between.

*Sound out the individual words.

*Link them to each other in groups separated by punctuation points.

*Recite the linked sections as you go along.

*Begin each learning block by recapping what you've learned so far.

CHAPTER 10
COMPETITION

Earlier in this book I've used the phrase 'learning to be better' as an actor. I deliberately avoided saying 'Better than everyone else'. This form of competition is poison to the soul and is a greedy ogre of the external that can never be pleased. Obviously, when you're being considered for a part there is usually only one to be had and you want to gain it instead of another person. However, remove any negative thoughts about the other auditionees. Their performance and chances are *nothing to do with you*. Your attention is solely focused on generating your very best in the most positive manner to get that job. You can't do that fully and allow unpleasant thoughts about the other innocents in the running. Aside from the greater humanity of being generous, competition with others creates a tight, tense and mean attitude in your meeting and reading. Be happy. Be healthy. Be employed.

The only form of competition you will ever gain from profoundly is in improving your own development compared to who you were yesterday. You can feel it, nurture it and appreciate the progression. That's evolution, and it's a vital part of why we are here. If you're locked onto simply besting an opponent, all that teaches you is who you are in relation to them. Making someone else your benchmark to beat may actually be setting your personal bar too low.

If you are true to climbing your own personal mountain of achievement rather than judging by comparison to others, your performance will naturally excel to much greater heights even if you are placed seemingly in direct competition with others. Some years ago, the L.A. Lakers basketball team won a season's Championship title against the odds. Critics unfairly perceived their victory as a fluke, dismissing them as soft, glamorous friends of the Hollywood set rather than serious athletes. In his book about the next season, the Lakers' coach set himself the fascinating question: "How do you motivate a winning team to prove themselves all over again?" His shrewd answer was to ignore outside competition and focus each player on improving individual targets in every aspect of their current game, irrespective of the teams they were to play, whilst still maintaining the vital sense of teamwork. This personal mission was instilled in each man and took the team to their second successive title win, silencing the naysayers and their opponents.

You're going to be around yourself a long time so invest in self-mastery, becoming comfortable with yourself, asking the best of your inner nature. Another wonderful thing about competing only with you is that even if the job doesn't work out, you can still come away feeling like a winner. If you know you improved in some way, such as overcoming nerves or listening more to direction, then that can be a source of self-esteem. Gloom and despondency are hard to allow in when you are raring to build on that new learning next time.

CHAPTER 11
AGE CANNOT
WITHER YOU

Ignore limited thinking based on your age. There is a terrible propaganda which says "If you haven't made it by thirty, you never will". This was told to me by an agent of mine who soon became an ex-agent. She had obviously never heard of Gene Hackman, Clint Eastwood and many more that learned their craft quietly before becoming known only after their youth. Prominent actors such as Nigel Hawthorne and Morgan Freeman came to household name recognition after they reached middle-age.

Actors who want to become a 'name' succeed from different choices and opportunities taken at different times in their career. There's no time limit or cut-off point by which you are supposed to have reached a certain level. Contrary to the perceived ageist anxiety around us, life is not a race and in our profession it is not all over by a certain point in your life. Such mental limitations to me say more about the speaker than the reality of the world.

For some performers, their looks and personality take a certain age before they gel. Somehow the package of their inner and outer selves fits congruently and they suddenly seem to become 'cast-able'. At my drama school years ago, one of the teaching faculty told student Gwen Taylor that she would achieve success, yet it would be later in her career rather than in her youth. Whoever told her this was absolutely right. It took some time before this actress's biological age and character suddenly seemed to work together and her television comedy career took off.

It always amuses me when the subject of retirement comes up. Actors work in a wonderful business that's not hide-bound by the need to escape from it in our sixties into such an idea. For most people, their jobs are a necessary function of financing their daily expenses until they can eventually afford to stop work. Health permitting, an actor can continue working in the field of their passion as long as they wish, denying the whole idea of retirement. If you're fortunate enough to have a career in the thing you love doing, why stop? In his nineties, Sir John Gielgud was not only still acting in high-profile film work, he continually called his agent every week asking what was coming up for him!

CHAPTER 12

LUCK

U p to now I've demonstrated how much I believe we are in the driving seat of our acting career. I hope this book has given you inspiration and removes some of the self-imposed limits that so easily prevent us from reaching our potential. The beauty of living with a firm game plan as I am suggesting is that it's a solid enough framework to allow for minor detours, hiccups and even the helping hand of what appears to be coincidence or good fortune.

Inevitably on any bold journey off the beaten track we may encounter some strange folk. So far I'm confident we've foiled most of the dangerous ones – yet there's one more I'd like to warn you about. He's a persistent and seductive serpent with two heads. Both of them will try to seduce you off the road with the same suggestion:

"It's plain and simple luck that decides whether or not you'll succeed, that's all. Forget making plans."

Perfomers who spout this fall into two categories. There are the Defeatists who believe that the world is a rigged card game where unless we have a sudden mysterious table visit by Lady Luck we cannot possibly win. In other words, what *we* do counts for nothing. Sharing this view of the importance of luck but for a different reason are the Fantasists. They have more in common with us since they are in a sense following their dreams. However, these are passive woolly-minded souls who fill their heads with accounts of their idols' stunning good fortune and imagine the same will happen to them with minimal effort because 'It could happen to me too'.

Both of these viewpoints are deluded. I'd like to discuss this magical Lady Luck a little further. Indulge me if you would by continuing to think of her as an elegant and much sought-after beauty. I don't believe her appearances from player to player are quite as random as they say, and woe betide anyone who takes her for granted. I also feel her unpredictability is part of her charm and need never be taken personally if she happens not to be at our side at times. Like many, she prefers to be courted by confident suitors whose positivity and drive attract her respect. The needy and resentful who offer excuses that 'I'd be successful too if only I had *her* by my side" have no-one to blame for their status but themselves. As for the candy-floss dreamer next to him, his blissful ignorance is rather sweet yet could never be taken seriously as a partner in the game of life.

Of course we face unexpected situations at times and they aren't always welcome, but we enhance our chances and create our own good fortune by how we work and think. The

Oxford English Dictionary defines luck as 'Success or failure apparently brought by chance' (so even they're hedging their bets in the use of that word 'apparently'). Other pithy definitions once more from the world of gambling variously describe it as 'an imaginary substance' believed to influence winning 'rather than the use of skill'. I couldn't put it better myself.

The 'reality' check

Be tolerant toward those who feel they are doing you a favour in warning you about your slim chances of success. They want what they feel is best for you, but haven't taken into account what I'm assuming - that you've already given yourself a good sober talking-to with or without my help and don't need to be patronised. When it's the turn of critics within our own ranks to dismiss our dreams harshly, it's usually because they've dismissed their own. Opinions like this can be diplomatically ignored. Defeatists justify their reasons for giving up by quoting stories about fellow actors whose route to fame seemed to hinge on a wildly implausible moment of sheer chance - a meeting, replacing an ill lead, discovery on the street etc. To them such tales are trump cards that 'prove' we are blindly optimistic hostages to fortune and should straighten up and get a steady job.

When you look beneath the surface of these anecdotes though, they often have a common detail that actually supports the argument that the benefactor is in the right place at the right time *on purpose.* The canny actor knows what they're doing and the direction they're going in even when the result isn't yet plain to see. The chorus girl who steps in to play the lead role when the star is injured is given a terrific sudden opportunity for advancement - it's certainly fortunate for her - but she wasn't in this crucial spot by accident. Her talent and dedication got her there in a prime position ready to be promoted when her moment came.

As for 'discovery', yes there is the age-old exceptional story of Lana Turner. Her journey could serve as a double-edged sword brandished by Defeatists and Fantasists alike. She was catapulted to fame after a well-connected Hollywood publisher saw her having a lunchtime coke at Schwab's Drugstore in Los Angeles. On the one hand this surely qualifies as freak professional luck. On the other hand it can't be given undue credence when you examine the true circumstances. Ms Turner was actually a trainee typist whose family moved to Los Angeles for the climate, not to pursue movie stardom, so her delirious rocket-trip to fame supports neither the cynics nor the dreamers' claims. Having said that, it could be argued that in a glamour industry town like the 'City of Angels', having your powerful figure spotted by an even more powerful figure could happen at any time. She was certainly living in the right place at the right time for such a coincidence to come her way.

Since you clearly want a self–supporting career as an actor a lot of your choices will be deliberately designed to help this. Basing yourself in the best location for your chosen industry is one part of the design, (remember we examined the dilemma of where to live in the 'Agents' chapter). Since Hollywood is the most visibly competitive arena in our profession, it's important to understand how few actors actually come from this small area. Instead they are imports, guided missiles homing in on Tinseltown from all over the world *on purpose*. When they happen to meet the right contact, hear of the perfect audition or struggle for years to become an 'overnight success', the foundation for their opportunities was already consciously laid.

'You're too kind...'

What also makes outside forces harder to downplay is when our prominent colleagues act as unofficial public relations representatives for them. Deliberate career planning of any kind is always left out when name actors review their achievements in interviews. As I said in the introduction, they will draw a veil over all their keenly focused hard work, preferring instead to express gratitude for 'being lucky'. Naturally, they should honour their good fortune - only a rude ingrate would take sole credit. At the same time they never forget they have an image to protect and don't want to appear immodest. Equally, if they project mystery or sexy rebelliousness it's harder for audiences to buy into this when they know their idol's fame came not from a sprinkling of star-dust or 'bucking the system' but from discipline, toil and a little 'ass-kissing' on the way up.

Unfortunately this slightly deceptive testimony is accepted as the truth by pessimistic and starry-eyed colleagues further down the ladder. They look at their own lack of results downheartedly and conclude they must be the victims of bad luck. As if the concept of luck doesn't brainwash enough, they now feel under pressure that if they haven't the good variety, it means they're cursed with the bad. Consequently a crushing unnecessary disillusionment sets in and many will then look for what seems an easier life.

What does this mean for you? All I suggest in bringing this book to a close is that you rely more on your own inner judgement as a confident determining factor in your success than outside forces. We can agree with both the Defeatists and the Fantasists that happy coincidence and chance do happen. Where we part company with them is that rather than join either camp in overly trusting or mistrusting luck, we actually trust *ourselves* first and invite luck in.

Install yourself in the most encouraging environment, inhabit the healthiest mental 'place' you can create, know what you desire and faithfully use all the tools you now have to build *your* reality. The world will obey how you view it. Let great opportunities meet great preparation.

It goes without saying then that the grand Lady herself will always have a seat readily reserved at your side and an open invitation to join you. Who could refuse?

~ I wish you the best of luck – and the best of work. ~

Lightning Source UK Ltd.
Milton Keynes UK
01 September 2010
159301UK00002B/2/A